RECIPES FROM THE CHÂTEAUX OF

Burgundy

Gilles du Pontavice

Bleuzen du Pontavice

Series editor:
BLEUZEN DU PONTAVICE

PHOTOGRAPHS
CLAUDE HERLÉDAN
Translation
ENTREPRISES 35

EDITIONS OUEST-FRANCE
13, rue du Breil, Rennes

he court of Duke Philip the Good of Burgundy was the most magnificent in Europe. Burgundy was rich in the 15th century, but doubly so because the duchy of Burgundy had been within the sphere of influence of the kings of France for centuries, whilst the lands of the Count of Burgundy formed part of the Holy Roman Empire. Philip could have been king of Friesland or Brabant, but a Duke of Burgundy did not need any other crown.

The meals at his court were lavish, and the wine good. The greatest Flemish painters thronged there, as Flanders, Artois, Holland, and Luxemburg all belonged to Burgundy When he crowned Louis XI as king of France, Duke Philip brought to the throne the man who was going to break up Burgundy, and to join part of it to France once again, as Charles the Bold, Philip the Good's son, was no match for Louis XI. The duchy passed to Charles' daughter, Mary of Burgundy, who married Maximilian, son of the Holy Roman Emperor, but to no avail, as in 1479, Louis XI annexed the Duchy of Burgundy to France. Eleven years later, this same Maximilian, then married by proxy to Duchess Anne of Brittany, was to abandon the second of the great independent duchies to the kings of France.

However, Burgundy, like Brittany, has never forgotten its golden age. There was a sudden break in its history, and now it is almost forgotten that the grandson of Marie of Burgundy and the Emperor Maximilian was prouder of his title of Count of Burgundy than that of Holy Roman Emperor. His name was Charles V.

It is said that Burgundy is a land through which people passed, and that its present-day borders are different from those that history had given it. We ourselves have found in the course of our travels around the châteaux that it has its own identity and soul. Obviously, there are the recipes and culinary tips, since that is object of this series. There is the real, generously-proportioned country cooking which embraces the shapes of its landscapes and the velvety texture of its wines. But it is also a certain assurance stemming from the landowning class in their châteaux where the same family has lived for centuries, whatever the problems and turmoil of the world around them.

In contrast to other regions, the châteaux in Burgundy are frequently a focal point of a village. Their chapel is sometimes the church, and they are highly visible and much visited. They once

Gougères are eaten at the wine-tastings in the cellar.

used to give shelter to the entire village population during the periods of apparently never-ending fighting, but are now peaceful sentinels, with their walls demolished, and their doors now open to visitors.

However, we also visited other places which are not châteaux, but which seemed to us to be very characteristic of this region. These were the Hôtel-Dieu in Beaune, which was built as a hospital for the poor, Clos de Vougeot, which is a celebration of the glory of wine, and Vézelay, which was a gateway from the West to the East and also part of the pilgrimage route to Santiago de Compostella.

Such is the portrait that is drawn of a Burgundy that is just as complex as its vineyards, where the monks were the overlords and where the favour of the vineyard owners is now courted. In short, a mosaic of country areas united by a single common spirit.

Michelet used to write, 'No part of France is more sociable than Burgundy.' We have found this in the earth that has never ceased to be listened to and cultivated, and in the treasures that it has never ceased to give us. From the 12 stages of our journey, punctuated, as was our duty, by a Burgundian fanfare in honour of the vineyards of the Côte-d'Or, we brought back impressions of a multifaceted, but unique Burgundy. It is now your turn to discover it. It is well worth the effort!

The celebrated Burgundian tastevin is primarily a tool for examining the colour and clarity of wine.

Clos de Vougeot

Noah, Bacchus, St Vincent, and all the others…

One of Clos de Vougeot's huge winepresses. Each one weighs 12 tons, is fixed down by 3 metre-deep piling, and could press 4 tons of grapes thanks to its screw that was worked by six monks.

It is impossible to write about the châteaux of Burgundy without stopping at Clos de Vougeot, and besides, all roads lead here. It stands imposingly above its famous vineyard, to which whole armies of visitors come to pay homage. This château's owner is the wine of the Clos, which was built with the sole intention of making wine from the grapes harvested by the Cistercian monks of Cîteaux Abbey, which was founded in 1098 by Robert de Molesme in order to re-establish links with the Benedictine Order. Jean-François Bazin, in a book dedicated to the Clos, has described the work of the monks exceptionally well. 'The men grouped together by St Bernard are neither fat or easy-going, but are really God's madmen, thin, hard, and fanatical. Right in the middle of their work, they stop to praise the Lord and then start digging again ten times as vigorously. [...] How could it be forgotten that the Clos Vougeot had its origins in this complex, but essentially spiritual, religious fervour, and that it is primarily a work of faith and an act of grace?'.

Cîteaux was very quickly given the vineyards at Vougeot, and then other gifts followed, the monks not resting until they had put an extensive wine estate together. The boundary walls of the Clos were constructed in the 14th century, but, because of its distance from the monastery, the Clos was in need of a wine-making room and a cellar, the first buildings of which date from the 12th century. With the passage of time, the strictness of the Cistercian Order was relaxed to allow some compromises, and in the 16th century, a country residence for the abbot of Cîteaux was built next to the wine-making room.

In 1791, Clos de Vougeot and its château became national property, and after several high bids, was sold in its entirety to Jules Ouvrard. After his death, however, the splitting up of the vineyard began, with the result that today it is divided between about 80 owners, of whom some have only a few rows of vines.

The 5 metre-wide fireplace in the kitchen.

The wine itself is not uniform in taste, which depends on the care taken in cultivation and the situation of the vineyards. Clos de Vougeot wine today is dark in colour, with a 'bouquet' of violets, rich and full-bodied. It is a wine which must absolutely be allowed to mature.

The Clos has survived various epidemics as well as the devastation caused by the plant-louse, phylloxera, whereas the château has survived history. After the splitting up of the Clos, it was bought, along with a quarter of the vineyards, by Léonce Bocquet, at whose death, it was sold to Etienne Camuzet, another important Burgundian merchant. Since 1944, it has belonged to a society made up of several prominent wine-growing families,

or, more correctly, a long lease has been granted to the Confrérie du Tastevin (Brotherhood of the Wine-tasting Cup), which is, in fact, the finest, the most impressive, and the most famous showcase for the wines of Burgundy.

'Le porteur de Bénaton', a sculpture by Henri Bouchard, stands in a prominent position in the cloister round which stand the winepresses and vinification rooms.

This evening, it is the 'Chapitre de l'Equinoxe' (Assembly of the Equinox), which, as usual, is preceded by a ceremony during which several new members join the Confrérie, thereby swelling the ranks of the 10,000 chevaliers (knights) of the Tastevin.

'By Noah, father of the vine
By Bacchus, god of wine
And by St Vincent, patron-saint of wine-growers,
We dub you a knight of the tastevin'.

The 12th century well has been dug directly into the chalk.

In front of 'le têtu' (the stubborn one), which is one of the huge 12th century wine-presses, a vine stock is lowered onto the chevalier designate's shoulder, after which everyone is briefly reminded of the qualities that make him a worthy recipient of such an honour. That particular evening, a Canadian restaurateur, who serves quail stuffed with caribou, a Japanese cookery teacher, and several Californians were dubbed 'chevaliers', the Californians being addressed with 'Dear Americans, you come to us from a country from which came phylloxera that destroyed our vineyards, and then Prohibition which ruined our wine-growers. Fortunately, after the disasters, you provided the remedies, first, young American vines, and then 'the French paradox.''

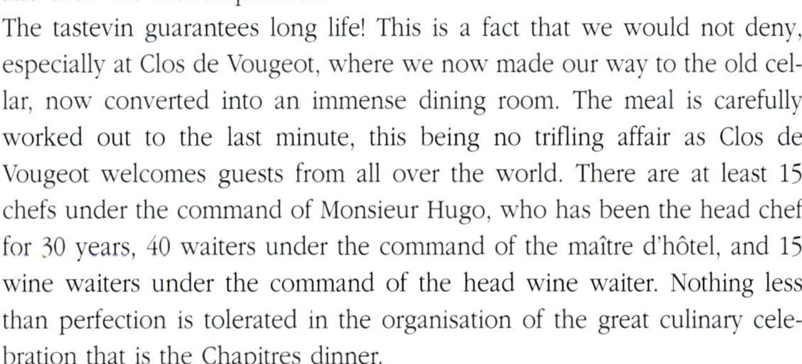

The tastevin guarantees long life! This is a fact that we would not deny, especially at Clos de Vougeot, where we now made our way to the old cellar, now converted into an immense dining room. The meal is carefully worked out to the last minute, this being no trifling affair as Clos de Vougeot welcomes guests from all over the world. There are at least 15 chefs under the command of Monsieur Hugo, who has been the head chef for 30 years, 40 waiters under the command of the maître d'hôtel, and 15 wine waiters under the command of the head wine waiter. Nothing less than perfection is tolerated in the organisation of the great culinary celebration that is the Chapitres dinner.

In the kitchen, everyone bustles about, just as they did in the 17th century. Sauce stocks simmer, fishes are steamed, eggs are poached ready for 'oeufs en meurette', game is prepared to be served 'à la poivrade' with peppery vinaigrette sauce, frogs' legs are baked, vols-au-vents are filled with crayfish, quail are prepared 'en chartreuses', small veal steaks are partnered with morel mushrooms, soft fruits are baked in a charlotte, and the snails are glazed. We are not going to reveal the secrets of these recipes here, because, as Monsieur Carlier, the great organiser of this magical mixture of word and wine, says, 'You must come to Clos Vougeot at least once in your lifetime.'

Menu of the meal

of the 857th Chapitre of the Chevaliers du Tastevin, 26th September 1998 to mark the Equinox

Baked frogs' legs in verjuice (the acid juice of unripe grapes), accompanied by a lively and vigorous Burgundy Aligoté 1996

Pike-perch with crayfish, escorted by a noble Chassagne-Montrachet Les Chaumées 1990

Poached eggs in a red wine sauce 'in the style of the wine-grower' (with grapes, vine leaves, wine, marc — a brandy distilled from the pressed grapes left over from wine-making — or brandy, moistened with a full-bodied Côtes-de-Nuits Villages 1998

Fillets of quail, braised with cabbage, bacon, and sausage, and served turned out of a mould with vegetables, washed down with a distinguished and velvety Volnay-Caillerets 1991

Fine cheeses from Burgundy and elsewhere, enhanced by a Mazis-Chambertin of aristocratic lineage

Boutehors, escargot en glace, a charlotte of soft fruits served in a tastevin, petit fours

Black coffee, aged marc, and prunelle (sloe gin), just the job for stimulating gentle mental activity

The coat-of-arms of the Confrérie du Tastevin includes a ruddy-faced Noah.

Rully

A château surrounded by its vineyards

80 square metres large and 7.50 metres high: these are the impressive dimensions of Rully's kitchen, which occupies the entire ground floor of the keep. The Montessus coat-of-arms is carved above the 16th century fireplace, on each side of which stand stone pillars carved with capitals of 'Burgundy cabbages'.

Four names altogether have made the history of Rully, which has never been sold. A keep was constructed in the 12th century by the lords of Rully, whose last heiress, Isabelle, married Robert de Saint-Leger in about 1370. The occupancy of this family saw the building of three round towers, including a dovecote, followed, in the 15th century, by living quarters which were erected against the surrounding wall. The château was thus well-defended with its path for the sentries behind the battlements, its protective dry moat, its bridge, and its drawbridge.

The enclosed vineyard situated in front of the château produces 'La Bressande' 'premier cru' white wine.

An attractive 'tastevin', with a handle in the shape of a coiled serpent.

This coat-of-arms has been designed to represent the château of Rully's history. From the top downwards are the arms of Rully (before 1370), of Montessus (from 1617 to 1927), and de Ternay (from 1927).

Moreover, a head made of leather has been found, the purpose of which was to fool an attacker as to the number of defenders.

In 1617, Charles de Saint-Léger's grandson brought Rully into the Montessus family, who were responsible for the construction, in 1716, of the outbuildings in the great courtyard, which are covered with large unfixed slabs of lava. The weight of this is immense, and so, accordingly, is the supporting timber framework.

In 1927, with her marriage to Count Jacques d'Aviau de Ternay, Edith de Montessus de Rully gave Rully its fourth name. The de Ternay family, which is wholeheartedly involved in wine-growing, is the present owner of the château.

Charles de Saint-Léger's glass. This 16th century glass is incredibly light and holds 3 litres of good Rully wine, and, as such, has long been used as a test for the family's future sons-in-law.

he château of Rully's cellar lies under one of its wings, and this gem of the 'Côte Chalonnaise' is just as much at home with its strong and full-bodied Chardonnay white wines as it is with its red Pinot Noir wines. The château's vineyard has been well-known for over 300 years.

After the grape harvest, the grapes are removed from the stems and then put into a vat to enable the colour and the tannins to be extracted from the grape skins. The length of this fermentation process varies according to the characteristics and quality of the vintage, and its effect is to transform the sugar of the grapes into alcohol. The wine is then decanted and left to mature, either in barrels or tanks. The remaining 'marc', or grape residue left after wine-pressing, is pressed in order to give 'vin de presse', of which all or part is added to the wine of the first pressing, which is called 'vin de goutte' (wine of the drops), because it flows freely from the grapes. The wine-making process then includes a second, or malolactic, fermentation, because it involves the breaking down of the malic acid to form lactic acid, the wine then being left to mature before it is bottled. The nurturing of a wine, like that of children, demands both time and constant care.

The vinification of white wines is more straightforward, as, since neither colour nor tannins are factors in the process, the grapes are pressed after being harvested.

After the lean years that followed the Second World War, the vineyard has been upgraded by Christian de Ternay. The wines from the château's cellar come from the best parts of the estate's vineyards, and are partly matured in new barrels, which produces a more complex wine.

The lees, or dregs, of wine, the heavy residue of the wine-making process, form an excellent basis for the sauces used in Burgundian cuisine, which makes ample use, both of wine and of the lees, in its recipes.

The traditional dual tap enables the wine to be bottled smoothly.

HOW TO MAKE 'RAISINET'

This recipe is taken from a very old cookery book at the château. Take the required quantity of grapes, remove the stalks, and then squeeze them gradually into the cauldron in which they are to be cooked over a high heat. As they boil, take out as many pips as you can with a skimmer, and reduce the liquid to a third, turning down the heat as it thickens. Taking care not to be burned, empty the grapes out of the pan and then sieve them through a white cloth, squeezing them hard with the hands. Having done that, return them to the heat, and stir the mixture constantly until it begins to boil. Remove it from the heat and put it immediately into a bowl. When it is warm, put the mixture into jars and leave them uncovered for 5 or 6 days, when they can be covered with paper. Check the 'raisinet' from time to time, and if the paper goes mouldy, take it off and replace it with some more. Continue this until the moisture has evaporated. The 'raisinet' will not go mouldy and spoil if it has been well cooked. If this is not the case, cook it a little again, before re-covering.

Poached eggs in red wine sauce.

Family recipes from Rully

POACHED EGGS IN RED WINE SAUCE

from Marie-France de Ternay

For 5 people:
10 eggs, 100g fatty bacon, 100g streaky bacon, 1 carrot, 1 onion, 1 clove of garlic, 1 bouquet garni, 2 to 3 tablespoonfuls flour, 1 tablespoonful butter, 100g small mushrooms, 1 cup meat stock, 5 croutons (slices of French bread, toasted or fried and rubbed with garlic), parsley, salt, ground black pepper, and 'Château de Rully' red wine.

Meurette sauce: the night before, make a 'pot-au-feu' (boiled beef with vegetables and beef broth), and keep back a cup of beef broth. Dice the fatty bacon and lightly fry in a sauté pan until the fat runs. Finely chop the carrot and onion, and stew it in the bacon fat (this is called a 'mirepoix'). Add the bouquet garni, cover, and leave to cook gently for 10 minutes. Add the red wine. Season. Bring to the boil, and add the beef broth and crushed garlic. Cook for 20 minutes over a high heat. Sieve the sauce into a largish deep dish, like a gratin dish. Crumble together the butter and flour and use to thicken the sauce. Check the seasoning.

Poaching of the eggs:
Simmer the sauce over a low heat. Break the eggs one by one directly into the dish and onto the sauce. They must not touch each other. Cook until the white becomes opaque. In the meantime, sauté the diced streaky bacon and the mushrooms. Prepare the croutons. Garnish the eggs and the sauce with the diced bacon, mushrooms, croutons, and a little chopped parsley.

LOBSTER BISQUE AND PIKE DUMPLINGS

from Brigitte de Ternay

A quick and easy recipe:
For 6 people:
12 ready-cooked quenelles de brochet (small pike dumplings), a 20 cl pot of crème fraîche, a tin of lobster bisque soup, 2 soup-tinfuls of milk, grated Gruyère cheese, and some margarine or unsalted butter.

Heat the oven to 250°.

Put the quenelles in a greased baking dish, and pour over the lobster bisque, the 2 tinfuls of milk, and the crème fraîche. Heat until simmering, stirring constantly.

Pour it over the quenelles until they are just covered. Sprinkle generously with grated Gruyère cheese. Let it rise in a hot oven for 25 to 30 minutes.

(Do not put the quenelles too close together in the dish, as they need room to rise.)

LA CUISINIERE BOURGEOISE, SUIVIE DE L'OFFICE. A l'usage de tous ceux qui se mêlent de dépenses de Maisons. Contenant la maniere de dissequer, connoître & servir toutes sortes de Viandes. NOUVELLE ÉDITION, Augmentée de plusieurs ragoûts des plus nouveaux, & de differentes Recettes pour les Liqueurs.

A BRUXELLES, Chez François Foppens, Imprimeur-Libraire.

M. DCC. LXXI.

This recipe book dates from the 17th century.

An old verjuice press, used to squeeze the juice from unripe grapes.

BEEF AND CARROTS IN A CHÂTEAU DE RULLY WHITE WINE SAUCE

For 4 people:
1kg piece of shoulder of beef, shin of beef, chuck steak, or top of rump of beef, 50g butter or margarine, 1 onion,
1 tablespoonful of flour,
1kg of carrots, 1 bouquet garni of parsley, thyme, and bay leaves, 1 teaspoonful of sugar,
3 glasses of Château de Rully white wine, 3 glasses of water, salt and pepper.

Peel and slice the carrots. Heat 50g of butter or margarine in a casserole, and brown the whole of the piece of meat over a high heat. Add the diced onion, and sprinkle with the flour, mixing well and leaving to brown for a minute. Add the carrots, and pour in the water and wine. Add the salt, pepper, and sugar, and mix together. Add the bouquet garni, and cook over a very low heat for 3 or 4 hours.

MARINADED WILD BOAR IN A RED WINE SAUCE

To make 4 litres of marinade:
4 litres of red wine, 2 bay leaves, 1 sprig of thyme,
10 juniper berries, 10 black peppercorns, 1 onion, 2 cloves, 1 liqueur glass of wine vinegar, 3 carrots, salt and pepper.

Beef and carrots in a château de Rully white wine sauce.

Marinade the piece of game for 3 days, stirring the mixture well from time to time.
Preheat the oven to 7. Grease the piece of meat and roast for 1/2 hour. During this time, begin to cook the marinade, and after an hour, filter off the herbs.
Carve the meat and add it to the sauce. Simmer for about 2 hours. Thicken the sauce with about 2 tablespoonfuls of cornflour mixed with a little cold liquid, and also, if desired, 2 spoonfuls of cream.
The same recipe can be made with pork, but this requires marinading for only 2 days.

REINETTE DU CANADA APPLE OMELETTE

For 6 people: 10 Reinette du Canada apples, 6 eggs, 25cl milk, 1 tablespoonful flour, 50g sugar, 100g butter, pinch of salt.

Thinly slice the apples, and sauté quickly with the butter. Break the eggs into a bowl, adding the flour, milk, sugar, and salt. Beat well.
Add the apples and stir in.
Put the omelette into a large saucepan, and cook gently without turning it over.
Slide the omelette onto a serving plate by folding it in half. Sprinkle with sugar and serve hot.

TIPSY CREAM

'Into a casserole, put 3 demi-septiers (an old measure, un septier = 8 pints) of white wine, the peel of 2 limes, a pinch of coriander, a little cinnamon, and 3 ounces of sugar. Boil gently for a good 15 minutes.
In another casserole, mix half a teaspoonful of flour with 6 egg yolks, and gradually pour in the boiled wine, when it has cooled down to warm. Sieve all this, and cook in a bain-marie.
When it is set, take it out, and leave it to cool until you are ready to serve it.'

Vanilla, chestnut, and chocolate cream.

Béatrix's chocolate cake.

BÉATRIX'S CHOCOLATE CAKE

'Some years ago, little Béatrix wanted to copy her big sister, Bénédicte, who makes delicious desserts.
She started to bake a chocolate cake, but... she forgot the milk and the flour!
However, the whole family thought that the cake was so delicious that today we only ever make this recipe.
This cake, cut up into little squares, is always a real success, for lunch or as part of a party buffet.
For 6 people:
5 eggs, 125g caster suger, 100g butter, 150g confectioner's chocolate, and butter or margarine to grease the cake tin.

Heat the oven to 200° or thermostat 6. Beat the egg yolks and sugar until the mixture turns white. Whisk the egg whites until very firm.
Melt the chocolate in small pieces (1 minute in a microwave), and then the butter on top of the chocolate (20 seconds). Mix the yolks and the sugar with the melted chocolate and sugar. Gently stir in the whisked egg whites to the mixture.
Grease a cake tin very well and pour in the cake mixture.
Cook for 25 minutes.'

VANILLA, CHESTNUT, AND CHOCOLATE CREAM

from Marie-France de Ternay

'This is a slightly thick vanilla cream, made with 1/2 litre of milk, a tin of creamed Ardèche chestnuts, and 1/2 a tablet of cooking chocolate.'

To make the vanilla cream, heat 1/2 litre of milk with a peeled vanilla pod.

Beat 5 egg yolks with 100g sugar until the mixture turns white, and then pour the heated milk onto it, stirring well. Heat again to a thick consistency.

Put a tablespoonful of creamed chestnut into small individual dishes, and pour the vanilla cream on top. To make the fondant topping, melt the chocolate together with the milk in the microwave.

Mix together until a smooth cream is obtained.

Decorate the dishes with the fondant topping. Serve cold.

TRADITIONAL QUINCE JELLY

Wipe the quinces, cut them in four, and remove any black skin. Take out the pips and put them to one side. Put the pieces of quince into a large pan, and add water to cover about 3/4 of them.

Tie the pips up firmly in a thin handkerchief, and put them into the pot. Cook for about an hour. The pieces of quince should be tender.

Take a linen teacloth which you do not mind being stained a little by the fruit, and put into it a small amount of the hot stewed quinces, rolling it up and holding it tight. (Take great care not to burn yourself).

When the juice runs out, press again, knead, unroll it a bit, and press again.

Scrape off the juice sticking to the outside of the teacloth with a spoon. Put the residue in the teacloth to one side for future use in the making of fruit jellies.

Repeat the operation until the stewed quince has all been used up.

Weigh the juice.

Add the same weight of caster sugar.

Cook this in a pan for about 3 or 5 minutes after it starts to boil fast. Skim. The jelly is cooked when it sticks to the edge of a spoon. Bottle.

QUINCE JELLIES

Once the quince jelly has been made, pass the purée through a vegetable mill. Weigh it and then weigh out a little less than the same weight in sugar (e.g. 2.9kg of sugar for 3kg of purée). Cook the mixture in a large pan on a medium to high heat for at least 15 minutes so that it bubbles fiercely, stirring constantly with a wooden spoon Wear a rubber glove because the purée tends to spurt out.

Stop cooking when the purée caramelises a little (it turns dark brown).

Pour the purée onto several dishes, and leave to dry uncovered.

Cover the dishes with a teacloth, put them in some cupboards, and forget about them for several weeks.

Cut the jelly mixture into small squares, roll them in caster sugar, and taste them. They can also be stacked into plastic boxes to be kept in the fridge until required.

The big 17th century oak table has a hollow in its surface for the crushing of nuts. The kitchen is filled with the aroma of Rully's quince jelly.

Fontaine-Française

A treasure casket

Fontaine-Française's private kitchen.

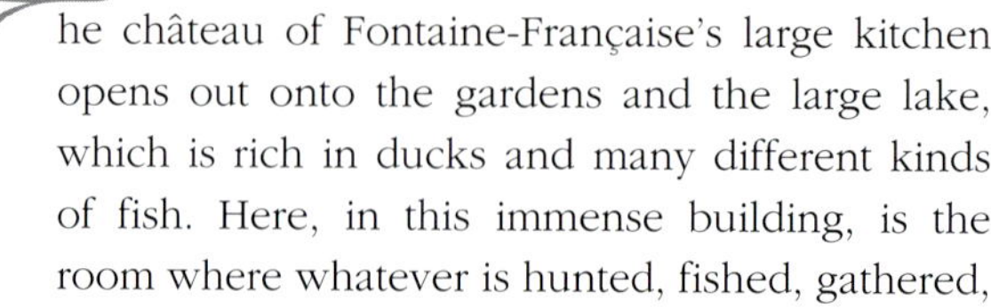

The château's private dining room, which looks out over the lake, as do the reception rooms. The family's children have their own little table there.

The château of Fontaine-Française's large kitchen opens out onto the gardens and the large lake, which is rich in ducks and many different kinds of fish. Here, in this immense building, is the room where whatever is hunted, fished, gathered, or cultivated on the estate is prepared and dressed for the table. It used to be the chapel of cardinal de Givry, but this moved to the first floor, and the kitchen has made itself at home, each century bringing it its own particular cooking facilities. There is a well for fresh water, a fish tank into which are put fishes from the lake, a bread oven in the fireplace, and a wood-burning cooker. There are large tables for the cutting up of meat, marble surfaces and mortars, and copper pots with the family's cipher. To complete the picture, we will add the heat of the ovens, the appetising smell of venison, and the stampeding of the children, Henri and Hadrien, through the rooms that run between the two wings.

Here, on the borders of Burgundy, Champagne, and Haute-Saône, used to stand an old fortress, an enclave of the kingdom of France within the powerful duchy of Burgundy. The name of Fontaine-Française has been famous ever since the battle of the same name, which took place on 5th June, 1595, when the dynamic French king, Henri IV, at the head of 900 cavalrymen, defeated the 12,000 men of the Duke of Mayenne and the king of Spain. The king, who had converted to Catholicism the year before, here put an end to the Wars of Religion, which had devastated the country, as well as strengthening his power.

This enormous boiler that was used for the washing of household linen stands in the kitchen. Although progress has rendered it obsolete, it is still an impressive piece of equipment.

The château was rebuilt between 1754 and 1758 by François Boullioud de Saint-Julien, who gained possession of it through his wife, Anne de la Tour de Pain. It looks very formal, even severe, from the outside, and the central portion gives the whole a certain air of grandeur which goes so well with the 18th century classical style. The tiled roof that covers the dormer windows reminds us that we are still in Burgundy, and the park planted with 400 trimmed lime trees provides a superb setting. It is said that the lime trees are the same age as the château, but in any case, they are very old. Trimming them each year is a major undertaking, but is necessary if the beauty of the whole group is to be preserved. There are also venerable old boxtrees, among which unexpected views are revealed within this park of surprises.

Fontaine-Française has often been handed down through the fema le line. Anne de la Tour de Pin welcomed Madame de Staël, Rousseau, and Voltaire here, but, having no direct heir, she left it to a niece. It then passed, without being sold, to the ruling family of Monaco, the Grimaldis, then to the Chabrillan family, and finally to Count Xavier de Caumont La Force, who welcomed us into his family in our search for recipes. The freshwater crayfish and fish come from the lakes, and the game and mushrooms from the forest. The château's cuisine plays its part in bringing the produce of its own estate to the table, where the formal meets up with the everyday.

Game and fish recipes

FRESHWATER CRAYFISH 'AU NATUREL'

There is no need to 'castrate' the crayfish, i.e. to remove the bitter-tasting gut, as long as they are not fed for two days before they are to be eaten. Prepare a court-bouillon as normal with thyme, bay leaves, and coarse salt. Throw in the crayfish and cook for 10 minutes at the most. Drain them and leave them to cool.
It is considered to be good manners to remove the shells with the fingers, but only for this recipe! For all other recipes, the shells are removed in the kitchen.
The wine to accompany this plain and simple crayfish dish will also be honest and natural, like a good, very dry Chablis, for example.

CARP IN A RED WINE SAUCE

Prepare a court-bouillon with red wine, and add carrots, onions, the fish head and tail, together with the roe, if there is any. Cook for half an hour. Cut the carp into slices. Sieve the court-bouillon, squeezing it all through.

Carp, pike, tench, and other white-fleshed fish abound in this region of lakes and rivers.

Replace on the heat and put in the pieces of carp. Cook for 20 to 30 minutes, during which time, prepare the soft-boiled eggs.
Make croûtons of buttered bread. Pour the carp and the sauce onto a dish, and garnish with the soft-boiled eggs and fried croûtons.
The flesh of the carp is strong enough to stand a good red wine. We see it going with a good Passetoutgrains, which is relatively low in tannin because of the Gamay grape.

WARM SPINACH SALAD WITH FRESH-WATER CRAYFISH

Peel the crayfish, keeping the shells and pincers to use in another recipe, e.g. bisque (a thick seafood soup) or sauce Nantua (a rich puréed crayfish sauce). Wash the spinach and remove the stalks, then cook the crayfish, tossing them in butter. Put to one side. Prepare a vinaigrette with chopped herbs (chives, chervil, and parsley), and mix with the spinach. Arrange on a dish, decorating it with crayfish tails.
We hesitated before recommending a suitable wine to go with this recipe, but why not a white Jura wine, made from the distinctive Savagnin grape, from the neighbouring region of Franche-Comté?

CHINESE CARP IN CHAMPAGNE SAUCE

Chinese carp is longer in shape than its cousin, the common carp, being a little – and here we hope to be forgiven – like a freshwater bass, and has become well acclimatised to Fontaine-Française's lakes.
After gutting and cleaning the fish, season the inside.
Preheat the oven.
Place the fish on a long plate, and wrap the head and tail in tin foil.
Pour half a bottle of champagne (reserving 2 soup spoons of it) onto the fish and coat with single cream.
Cook at first in a hot oven, and then lower the temperature for about 30 minutes, after which take out the fish, and remove the skin and tin foil.
Keep warm while making the sauce.
Strain the cooking juices through a sieve and into a small casserole. Beat over a high heat for 2 minutes, during which the juices and the cream will thicken.
Add the reserved champagne and beat, adding some pieces of well-chilled butter.
Check the seasoning.
Pour the sauce over the fish, or leave to serve in a sauce boat.
To accompany this dish, you will, quite logically, drink the same champagne.

MARINADED HAUNCH OF VENISON

The haunch of venison should be left to marinade the night before in some good red wine, seasoning, onions, and carrots.
Turn the piece of meat two or three times.
Preheat a very hot oven.
Remove the venison from its marinade and put in a large dish. Sprinkle it with some oil and put some pieces of butter on it. Sieve the marinade and pour a large glass of it onto the dish.
Put it in the oven. Allow a good hour's cooking time, basting the meat from time to time.
Make a roux of half flour, and half butter, and colour it over the heat.
Add the strained marinade and stir to thicken.
Clean the mushrooms (preferably 'girolles' or 'trompettes-de-la-mort'), and cook them in a large pan, starting with the 'trompettes', so that some of their moisture content can evaporate, and then the 'girolles'.
Sprinkle with chopped garlic and cook on a low heat.
When the venison is cooked, leave it to rest.
Pour the meat juices into the sauce, and add a little redcurrant jelly.
Stir well until smooth.
Carve the venison into slices, cover with the sauce, and serve with forest mushrooms.
This dish calls for a great Burgundy, full-bodied but elegant - Vosne-Romanée or Volnay.

RHUBARB TART

Make some pastry with 250 g of flour, an egg yolk, a pinch of salt, a spoonful of oil, 100g of sugar, and 100g of butter melted in a bain-marie.
Spread it over a circle of greased paper that is a good centimetre bigger than the baking tin that you will then put it in, and let it rest for 1 hour.
Clean 6 sticks of rhubarb and cut into small pieces.
Put them on the pastry and scatter with a little sugar and with some knobs of butter.
Cook in a hot oven for about 30 minutes.

EGGS IN ASPIC

Put a little jelly, that you have already melted, into the bottom of a savarin cake tin, put in the soft-boiled eggs, and cover with jelly.
Put it in a cool place to allow the jelly to set.
Turn it out of the tin by putting it in hot water, using a knife to prise away the aspic.
Put a green salad in the centre of the ring. You can also add extra small decorative touches, such as diamond-shaped pieces of tomato or cucumber skin, and chopped black olives, to the first layer of jelly.

RASPBERRY ICE

For 6 people:
1 cup of sugar
2 cups of hot water
1/4 lb fresh raspberries
4 tablespoonfuls of orange juice
A pinch of salt

Cook the sugar in some hot water for 5 minutes. Purée the

raspberries by passing them through a sieve, and then add them to the sugar and water, together with the orange juice and the salt.
Leave to cool, and, when set, place in a freezing tray.
Beat it, put it back into the freezing tray, and leave to freeze.

STRAWBERRY MOUSSE

For 8 people:
1/2 lb strawberries
1 cup crystallised sugar
2 teaspoonfuls lemon juice
2 cups whipped cream
2 egg whites
A pinch of salt

Wash and hull the strawberries, then add the sugar and crush them. Heat until the sugar has melted. Sieve and chill in the fridge. Add the lemon juice. Beat the egg whites, with a pinch of salt, until they form stiff peaks, and then add this mixture to the whipped cream. Place in a freezing tray or dishes, and freeze without stirring. Decorate with strawberries or whipped cream.

STRAWBERRY ICE-CREAM

Prepare a vanilla cream, and leave to cool.
Add a tablespoonful of lemon juice to a cupful of strawberries, and beat.
Then add the vanilla cream.
Beat together until smooth.
Put into a freezing tray, and into the freezer.

SAINT-FARGEAU

La Grande Mademoiselle

Saint-Fargeau's circular dining room.

It was a television series that revealed to France the death throes of a world that was so near in time and yet so far, a world of the aristocracy, hunts, and ancestral traditions that was swept away by the Great War and the telephone, the world of 'Au Plaisir de Dieu' (At God's Pleasure). Jean d'Ormesson recounted the end of a class which was no longer wanted by the modern world, and which also signalled the death knell of the château of Saint-Fargeau, which was too old, and too large (with its 365 windows!), and which was finally condemned to divided up. Neither the French state nor the department of the Yonne wanted it, but in 1979, two brothers, Michel and Jacques Guyot, bought it with the ambitious plan of restoring it and opening it to the public.

Since then, Saint-Fargeau has undergone a renaissance. Extensive restoration work has been undertaken, including the retiling of 2 hectares of roof, and the reconstruction of 'la Grande Mademoiselle's apartments, which had been destroyed in a fire in 1752. Today it is one of the main tourist attractions in Burgundy, and is the venue for an important historical pageant every summer.

Of course, life has changed, but Saint-Fargeau is still beautiful. We discovered here a long and eventful

The famous and impressive semi-circular staircase in the main courtyard leads to the chapel and the château's suites of rooms.

history, and tasted the recipes of the Puisaye region, which lies at the edge of Burgundy along the Loire valley.

There was a château here in about the year 1000, which was the property of the bishops of Auxerre, the first of whom was Héribert, the illegitimate brother of Hugues Capet, the French king. The next owners were the great noble family of de Toucy, all of whom went off to fight in the crusades. In 1255, Jeanne de Toucy, who was the last of her name, brought the estate with her on her marriage to Thibaut, Comte de Bar, in whose family, and that of its successors, the Montferrats, it remained until 1450.

The original oval portrait of the 'Grande Mademoiselle' was incorporated in the 19th century into a full-length portrait, such an alteration becoming established history.

It was bought in 1450 by Jacques Coeur, the king's powerful financier, and at Saint-Fargeau there is a Jacques Coeur tower, whose distinctive feature is that it has a hollow where rainwater can be collected. It seems, however, that he was not responsible for the alterations carried out to the château, which was then much more open than today, but which already had its curious five-sided design.

Antoine de Chabannes rebuilt the château after having bought it from King Charles VII in 1453. Despite having a few problems with King Louis XI – but then who didn't? – he achieved high governmental office, and constructed massive defences around the old château. Through the line of inheritance, Saint-Fargeau passed to the Anjou and then to the Bourbons Montpensier families. Henry de Bourbon was a close friend of Henri IV, and his only child, a daughter, was engaged to the king's son, the Duke of Anjou, the future Louis XIII's younger brother, but the marriage did not take place until 1626. The Duke of Anjou and Marie de Montpensier had a daughter, and what a daughter!

Anne Marie Louise d'Orleans, duchess of Montpensier, Saint-Fargeau, and Châtelleraud, countess of Bar-sur-Seine and Mortains, sovereign of Dombes, princess of La Roche-sur-Yon, and dauphine of the Auvergne, was born at the Louvre on 29 May, 1629. She was the niece of King Louis XIII and the first cousin of Louis XIV, and is better known by the name of the 'Grande Mademoiselle'. She was the heroine of tragic events for which Saint-Fargeau was the main setting.

Good fortune seemed to smile on her, as she was rich, richer, in fact, than anyone else in France. She should have married Louis XIV, but during the civil war of the Fronde (1648 – 1653), the great lords revolted in order to get rid of the intendants created by Richelieu, and to protect the wealth that they received from their estates. The king was then only 13 years old. The cardinal de Retz, the princes of Condé and Conti, and other important members of the nobility took up arms, Gaston d'Orleans and his 22 year old daughter among them. The 'frondeurs' were defeated several times. Condé, the governor of Guyenne, even enlisted the help of a Spanish army, but was defeated by Turenne at Blénau, near Saint-Fargeau on 1 April, 1652. Condé won Paris, whilst Louis XIV took refuge at Saint-Fargeau. Condé, arriving in Paris with his troops, pursued by the royal army, came up against the gates of the Faubourg Saint-Antoine, and it was Gaston d'Orleans who had them opened. The king's army, however, attacked the 'frondeurs', while the 'Grande Mademoiselle' ordered the firing of cannons from the Bastille on her illustrious cousin. There was never any question of marriage after that!

In October, 1652, Louis XIV returned victorious to Paris. The rebels had lost. In the wing of the Tuileries where she lived, the 'Grande Mademoiselle' received the order to 'move out of the Tuileries by tomorrow morning'. It was exile. Gaston d'Orleans ended his days at the château de Blois, whereas for his daughter, it was Saint-Fargeau, described thus in her Memoires, 'We arrived at Saint-Fargeau at 2 o'clock in the morning, and we had to get down and walk as the bridge was broken. I entered an old house that had neither doors nor windows, and with grass growing right up to the steps in the courtyard. I was horrified. I was led to a hideous room which had a post in the middle. Fear, horror, and sorrow gripped me, so much so that I began to cry. I felt so utterly miserable, what with being away from the Court, not having a more beautiful

place to live than that, and reflecting that this was the most beautiful of all my châteaux.'

Exiled, alone, but still rich, she decided to have the château restored, and settled down there, creating a provincial court. Handsome apartments were built, as well as a theatre.

'The pack of hounds and the many horses that I had sent for from England arrived. I began to hunt three times a week, which I thoroughly enjoyed. The area around Saint-Fargeau is beautiful hunting country, and just right for the English hounds, who normally go too fast for ladies.' In 1657, the king allowed her to return to Paris, where she moved into the Palais du Luxembourg. Among her countless other suitors, it was proposed that she should marry King Alphonso VI of Portugal, but she refused, and left Paris again to spend another period of exile at Saint-Fargeau.

In 1670, the 'Grande Mademoiselle' was no longer a young girl, but back in Paris, she fell in love with one of the king's officers, Antoine Nompar de Caumont La Force, count of Lauzun. The king agreed to the marriage, and then went back on his word. Lauzun was taken to the fortress of Pignerol, which he only left after 9 years, and at a high price for Mademoiselle, as in exchange, she had to give up the principality of the Dombes and the county of Eu to the king's children. Lauzun was freed, she gave him Saint-Fargeau, and they married in secret (this is sometimes disputed, which is perfectly normal for a secret). However, in 1685, the 'Grande Mademoiselle' separated from her husband, who did not love her, ill-treated her, and who held onto Saint-Fargeau. She turned to a life of religious devotion, and died in 1695. Saint-Fargeau was bought by a financier, Antoine Crozat, in 1715.

But that is another story. It is now time to sit down to a meal! Here are some of the recipes that we collected at Saint-Fargeau.

Saint-Fargeau's landscaped park provides many beautiful views across onto this large and impressive building.

Wherever did these deer's hoofs tipped with metal and made into table forks by an impish craftsman com from? We shall never know.

EGGS LULLY

It is said that one day, whilst in the Saint-Fargeau's kitchens, the Grande Mademoiselle found a young kitchen hand who was a gifted violinist, and who composed a simple song called 'Au clair de la lune' (By the light of the moon). She arranged for him to have lessons, and then introduced him to the Court. His name was Jean-Baptiste Lully.
'These are 'oeufs au plat', cooked in butter in a shallow dish in the oven with some table salt. On top of the eggs, put pieces of grilled sheep's kidneys covered in Périgueux sauce (a rich, strong brown sauce made of meat stock, and madeira or sherry, with truffle essence and chopped truffle)'.

CHICKEN WITH TRUFFLES AND ASPARAGUS

'Suprêmes' are poultry (generally chicken) fillets. Coat each chicken fillet with breadcrumbs by dipping them into some beaten egg, and then immediately into some breadcrumbs. Shake off any excess. Brown the fillets in a little clarified butter and leave to cook for 15 minutes. Arrange them in a ring on a dish, putting a thin slice of truffle on each one, and placing bunches of asparagus tips around them. Dot the fillets with 'beurre noisette' (brown butter with lemon juice and parsley).

TRIANGULAR CREAM CHEESE PASTRY

For 6 people: Flaky pastry made with 400 g flour, 300 g margarine (at room temperature), 20 cl water, and a pinch of salt.
Put the salt in the water, then stir in the flour until evenly mixed. Roll out the pastry, blending the margarine into it. Roll out the pastry to a thickness of about 5 mm. Fold one third over to the centre, then the other third over that, and then give it a quarter turn. Repeat the whole process five more times. Cut out 20 cm rounds of pastry.
Filling: 1.5 kg fromage blanc of either cow's or goat's (fresh soft cream cheese), 100 g grated Gruyère, 3 eggs, 12 g salt, 2 g white pepper with some grated nutmeg.
Put the drained and dried fromage blanc into a basin, and add the three eggs, Gruyère, salt, pepper, and grated nutmeg. Mix together. Place this mixture in the centre of each round of pastry, and then fold them in from three directions to form a triangular purse. Cook the corniottes for 30 minutes at 180°C.

Cream cheese tart.

BACON FRITTERS

6 eggs, 300 g wheat flour, 100 g buckwheat flour, 1 litre full cream milk, 2 tablespoons cider, 300 g bacon, 20 g salt.
Mix the 2 flours and then the eggs, salt, and pepper to a smooth paste in a bowl. Add the milk and stir continuously. Add the cider. Leave the batter to rest for at least an hour in a cool place. Cut the bacon into small pieces, brown in a frying pan, and then pour the batter over the bacon. Leave to cook, and serve hot with a main dish.

CREAM CHEESE TART

This a speciality of the Puisaye region of Burgundy.
Prepare some shortcrust or

flaky pastry, according to taste. Put some fromage blanc (cream cheese) into a bowl with 3 eggs, 2 or 3 spoonfuls of flour, salt, pepper, and grated nutmeg (optional). Mix well, pour into the pastry case, and cook in a hot oven for 40 minutes, or according to your oven.

BACON QUICHE

Prepare a shortcrust pastry case, and on it put some very thinly-sliced rinded bacon, arranged lengthways. Mix together 3 eggs, 20 cl crème fraîche, and a little milk, add some grated Gruyère, season, and pour into the pastry case. Cook in the oven until the quiche is nice and golden.

RABBIT IN CIDER

Cut the rabbit into several pieces, and brown them, piece by piece, over a high heat. Put to one side and brown some small bacon pieces. Lower the heat. Put in a little flour and 1/2 litre of cider. Add the rabbit pieces, and cook for 45 minutes. Season.
Stir, and then remove the rabbit pieces. Add some 'crème fraîche' to the sauce, and then some water to dilute. Pour the sauce over the rabbit. Peeled and sliced potatoes fried in butter go well with this cider dish.

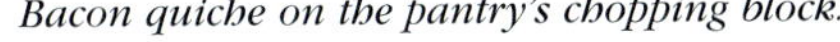

Bacon quiche on the pantry's chopping block.

Saint-Fargeau's history is linked with that of its forest teeming with deer, wild boar, and wolves, of which here is displayed a collection of their hoofs and feet.

VEAL OLIVES IN CIDER

Take 1 veal escalope per person, and put on it a little sausage meat stuffing. Roll up the escalope, bard with a thin slice of bacon, and tie with string. Brown in the frying pan in a little fat. Lower the heat, pour in a glass of cider or two, depending on the number of portions. Season, and cover to cook for 15 minutes. Remove the 'paupiettes', and add a little 'crème fraîche', or a knob of butter which is to melt gently. Cover the 'paupiettes' with the sauce.

GOAT'S CHEESE SALAD

For a light meal: wash and clean a lettuce of your choice. Crumble up a goat's cheese, and mix some finely chopped parsley and some finely crushed garlic with it.
Sprinkle on the salad tossed in vinaigrette.

Cormatin

La Varenne's kitchens

LE
CVISINIER
FRANCOIS,
ENSEIGNANT LA MANIERE
de bien apprester & assaisonner
toutes sortes de Viandes, grasses
& maigres, legumes,
Patisseries, &c.
Reueu, corrigé, & augmenté d'vn Traitté de Confitures seiches & liquides, & autres delicatesses de bouche.
Ensemble d'vne Table Alphabetique des
Matieres qui sont traittées dans
tout le Liure.
Par le sieur DE LA VARENNE, *Escuyer de Cuisine de Monsieur le Marquis d'Vxelles.*
TROISIESME EDITION.
A PARIS,
Chez PIERRE DAVID, au Palais, à
l'entrée de la Gallerie des Prisonniers,
au Roy Dauid.
M. DC. LII.
AVEC PRIVILEGE DV ROY.

The great workshops where La Varenne reigned supreme were replaced by the château of Cormatin's present kitchen during the Revolution.

To the high and mighty seigneur, my lord Louis Chaalon du Bled, councillor to the king in both the State and Privy Councils, Knight, Marquis d'Uxelles and Cormatin [...] During the 10 whole years that I have worked in your house, I have found the secret of the exquisite preparation of meats [...] It is why, my lord, employ your customary generosity, do not scorn it, although it is unworthy of you. Consider it to be a treasure of sauces, of which the taste has pleased you sometimes, which

The kitchen's 'potager', a large open wood-fired stove used for the cooking of soups.

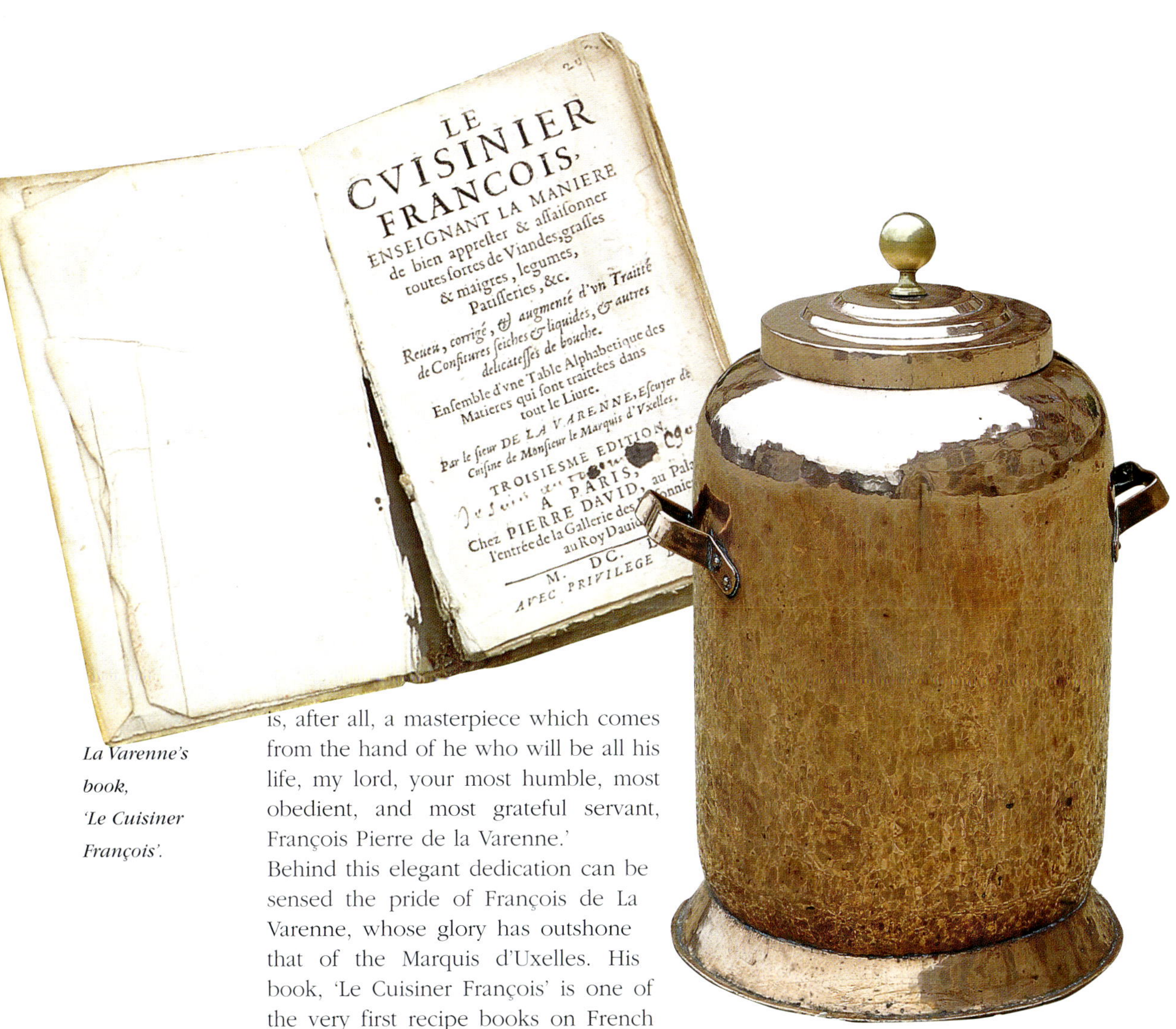

La Varenne's book, 'Le Cuisiner François'.

is, after all, a masterpiece which comes from the hand of he who will be all his life, my lord, your most humble, most obedient, and most grateful servant, François Pierre de la Varenne.'

Behind this elegant dedication can be sensed the pride of François de La Varenne, whose glory has outshone that of the Marquis d'Uxelles. His book, 'Le Cuisiner François' is one of the very first recipe books on French cooking. Here is expounded the art of meats and fishes, but also, among other things, that of jams and liqueurs, the art of the 'maître d'hôtel' who was in charge of the household, that of the 'écuyer-tranchant', who cut up, sliced, and trimmed the meat, and that of the 'sommelier', who looked after the wines, and who was then expert in the folding of table napkins.

This utensil is a charcoal extinguisher, and it connects the fireplace with the 'potager'. In it are put the embers from the household's wood fires, which, deprived of oxygen, are transformed into charcoal.

Today Cormatin's old kitchens, where La Varenne reigned supreme, have been abandoned. They used to be situated in the basement of the south wing, which was destroyed in 1815. This part of the building had been let to a cloth-manufacturer, who had the central staircase removed, as well as the two supporting walls. This caused the whole wing to collapse, opening up the château's outlook, but at the expense of the symmetry of its design. However, the kitchen had already been moved to the north wing, where it can be visited today. It is a huge, well-lit room, where there is a fireplace for the roasting spit, as well as a 'potager' (an open wood-burning stove for the cooking of soups), and a cast-iron stove with a inverted draught.

Recipes from the first edition of 'Le Cuisinier François' (1651).

FROGS' LEGS SOUP WITH SAFFRON

'Truss up your frogs' legs, & put them to boil with stock, or purée, & season with parsley, an onion studded with cloves, & a sprig of thyme. Simmer your bread, & put on it your white frogs' legs, with some saffron or egg yolks, & then serve.'

RASPBERRY SOUP

'Mix some milk with some raspberries, and sieve them together. Boil some milk, that has been well-seasoned with salt, & when it boils, throw in your mixture & stir well. Pour it out, decorate with raspberries, & serve.'

STUFFED PIKE

'Split it open along the back, & remove the skin from the head to the tail. Remove the flesh & small bones. Leave the spine so as to hold it firmer when stuffed. Then take 1/2 quantity of pike flesh & 1/2 quantity carp or eel flesh, chop finely with parsley, raw egg yolks, salt, pepper, a mixture of finely chopped herbs, butter & milk. Mix together, with some mushrooms, stuff your pike, sew it up, & then put it to cook in a dripping pan. Make your sauce with the fish stock or purée, a drop of verjuice, & a little vinegar, that you have strained into a pan with parsley, capers, & mushrooms, that you will season & cook thoroughly. Serve & garnish with whatever you want when it is well-cooked.'

FRIED EGG WHITES IN SYRUP

'Make a thick syrup, fry some egg-whites with some butter in a pan, & put them in your syrup. Serve them with some orange-flower water.'

NULLE

'Take a dozen egg yolks & two or three whites, put in a little cream, a little salt, & a lot of sugar. Beat the mixture well, & then strain through a sieve, & put it on a plate, or in a dish. When you are ready to serve, cook it on the stove, or in the oven, & when cooked, serve with sugar & scented water, & decorate with flowers.'

A table napkin folded in the form of a cock

'Fold a table napkin in half, in such a way that the two hems are together. Fold it along its length as small, as tight, & as low as you can. Roll it up small, while holding it tight. Open it out until one finger away from the centre. Fold up the pleats & hold it tightly. Put a large round loaf of bread in the centre of the folds. Place the edges of the napkin onto the bread. Pull up the head & the beak of the cock from the centre of the napkin, & make it a cockscomb, wattles, & eyes from some red cloth. You will make the end of the beak with a trimmed feather which you will hold in place with some tragacanth (plant gum) mixed with some orange water, or another scent. Pull out the tail from the other end, & raise it as high as you possibly can.'

Bon courage! I hope it goes well!

When you have mastered the art of folding napkins in the shape of a cock, you will be able to learn how to fold them into
'the shape of a hen with her chickens',
'the shape of two capons in a pie',
'in the shape of a hare',
or even 'in the shape of a dog with a collar'!

Two 'DUXELLES' recipes

'Duxelles' is a preparation of chopped mushrooms whose name comes from the Marquis d'Uxelles, as he too has his place in the history of food and drink. Here are two of the recipes that La Varenne dedicated to him.

MUSHROOM AND ONION PASTE (DUXELLES)

Sweat some finely chopped shallots and onions in butter. Finely chop some button mushrooms, and add to the pan. Cook at first on a high heat so that the water evaporates from the mushrooms, then on a low heat. Season, and at the end of the cooking, add some 'crème fraîche' (slightly soured cream);This is optional. This 'duxelles' mix can be used as a filling for many dishes. There are 'artichauts (artichokes) à la duxelle', 'tartelettes (tartlets) à la duxelle', 'navets farcis duxelles' (turnips with a 'duxelles' filling), etc.

PIKE-PERCH WITH A 'DUXELLES' STUFFING

Open the fish along the back to remove the central bone. Prepare a 'duxelle' (see above) with which you stuff the pike-perch. Sew up the pike-perch, and poach it in a strong fish stock to which some white wine has been added.

A cream jug.

Cormatin's history is linked with that of the du Blé family. The original château was replaced in the late 13th century by a fortified castle, on the site of the present château. Antoine du Blé, who was born in 1560, was a leading commander of the Catholic League during the Wars of Religion, before joining the Protestants under King Henri IV. Rich and privileged, he started the château's construction in 1605, in an architectural style that is more French than Burgundian, with its three main buildings built around three sides of a square and encircled by a moat. Although the château has kept certain defensive elements, such as the drawbridge, it borrowed a lot from the great architects of the period. The grand staircase in the north wing juts out of the exterior wall, thereby giving the building a greater degree of sophistication. While Cormatin was being rebuilt, the estate passed to Jacques du Blé, Antoine's son, who was made a marquis in 1618. He also saw action in battle, at Genoa, at La Rochelle, and in Savoy. His wife, Claude, was a rich heiress, and dedicated herself to the château's interior decoration, which is the glory of Cormatin and one of the finest Louis XIII interiors in existence. Walls and ceilings are painted in a wealth of brilliantly-coloured motifs of flowers and fruits, and everywhere there are sheaves of wheat (blé) and the motto 'Bonne est la haie autour du blé' (Good is the hedge around the wheat), an allusion to the family's power. Gradually, Cormatin became increasingly neglected by the du Blé family, who were spending more time at the royal Court, and was finally sold in 1766, passing into the ownership of Sophie, an illegitimate descendant of the de Blés. Sophie's daughter, Nina de Pierreclau, became famous because of her affair with Alphonse de Lamartine, by whom she had a son, Léon. This was also a extremely troubled time in the life of Cormatin, as Nina, abandoned by her husband and family, and financially ruined, was forced to sell the château to the Lacretelle family. Lamartine often came back to Cormatin to work on the château's archives or to organise his political activities. A Republican, a government minister in 1848, and an

The view from the gardens of the château's exterior and the restored moats.

unsuccessful opponent of Louis-Napoleon Bonaparte, his career was often played out on the steps of Cormatin.

Was this to be the end of the château? No, it was certainly not, as Cormatin's eventful history sprang back to life again in a most unexpected way. In 1898, the Lacretelle family sold the château and its estate to Raoul Gunsberg, who had been the director of the Monte Carlo opera house for 50 years, and who was also an art-lover. Gunsberg restored the château according to his own personal tastes, which favoured the Neo-Gothic style, and filled it with works of art, the paintings of Leonardo da Vinci, Titian, and Raphaël providing the setting for the wild parties of France's 'Belle Epoque'. So many princes and opera divas got together at Cormatin that it would be impossible to list them all. However, the beautiful Nellie Melba, whose immortality has been assured by the naming of a dessert after her by Escoffier, must be mentioned here.

Cormatin's rooms are decorated with elaborate and exquisitely-detailed wall-paintings.

Then, as often elsewhere, the Great War abruptly swept this period aside, taking with it the parties and the paintings.

One of France's oldest listed historical monuments fell into oblivion. The park became overgrown, and the roofs lost their tiles. Cormatin was forgotten, sold, and then sold again, until in 1980, three friends, Anne-Marie Joly, Marc Simonet-Langlart, and Pierre Almendros, who were looking for an old house to restore, bought Cormatin for a very reasonable price. However, this was only the entrance fee to the château, as they restored the park and the rooms, whose magnificent interiors had fortunately been preserved, and opened them to the public. For a long time, it had been thought that the panels of St Cécile's cabinet had been stolen, but they were only suffering from damp, hidden under the decaying varnish, and have now been restored. The moat has been dug deeper, the park has been cleared, and the various gardens, with their maze, flower beds, Baroque garden, follies, and, of course, a kitchen garden, have all been restored to their original state.

After wars, passions, and parties, Cormatin is alive again, this time at a gentler pace, but for the pleasure of a greater number of people.

This beautiful washbasin from the 'Compagnie des Indes' (the French equivalent of the East India Company) is rare because of its size. The exterior was decorated to order in a European style, whereas the Chinese artists who decorated the interior gave free rein to their imagination.

SAUTÉ OF VEAL WITH LEMON

Take a mixture of veal 'tendrons' (small strips of meat from a rib of veal) and of 'noix' (topside of veal) cut into small pieces. Brown them over a high heat, put them to one side, and put in the pan some thinly sliced onions that you cook until golden. Stir in a little flour, and add a little white wine and some chicken stock. Put the meat back in the pan, add a little sugar and the juice of 3 or 4 lemons. Season, and leave to cook for an hour. 10 minutes before the end of the cooking time, add some 'pleurote' mushrooms and some coriander. We drank an excellent white Givry from the Joblot estate with this dish.

Beautiful and superb estate for sale

'This estate, previously known under the ownership of the marquisate d'Uxelles and the baronetcy of Cormatin, in the department of Saône-et-Loire, and which offers, by its beauty, the elegance of the château, and the delights of its living accommodation, everything that a noble lord and a very wealthy family could desire [...].

The enclosed area of land, in the centre of which stands the château, has 9 hectares and 61 ares (100 m^2)of land. The small woods in the gardens are beautiful. They are encircled by a lovely river that is very rich in fish, and on the banks of which is a terrace planted with lime trees, longer than that of the Feuillants in Paris [...].

The climate here is very favourable, and as proof of this, there are tulip trees, catalpa trees, Japanese lacquer trees, etc., which have been grown from seeds, sown 20 years ago, that the present owner brought back from America, and which are now beautifully well-established [...].

The hunting and fishing on such a large estate offers a considerable variety of pleasures and resources.'

Sale notice of Cormatin in July, 1808.

APPLE TART WITH RHUBARB JAM

Make some pastry with
250 g flour, 125 g butter,
1 tablespoonful caster sugar,
1 teaspoonful salt.
Add as much water
as needed.
Roll out the pastry
and place in a tart dish.
On it spread 2 minced apples,
on top of which arrange
some finely sliced apples,
and then cover
with rhubarb jam.
Cook in a medium oven for
40 to 45 minutes. Serve with
whipped cream.

PEACH MELBA

Nellie Melba, the celebrated opera singer, was very fond of desserts, and so Auguste Escoffier, the then chef at the Savoy Hotel in London, dedicated this dessert to her.
In a small glass dish, put two balls of vanilla ice-cream., cover with peach cooked in syrup, and cover with raspberry purée.

PINEAPPLE WITH SPICED GINGERBREAD

Cut a pineapple into small cubes, and crumble 6 to 8 slices of spiced gingerbread. Brown the pineapple in some butter until nice and golden, and then add the spiced gingerbread crumbs. Add 2 or 3 tablespoons of runny acacia honey, flambé the whole lot in rum, and allow to go dry but without burning.
Serve with some whipped cream Chantilly.

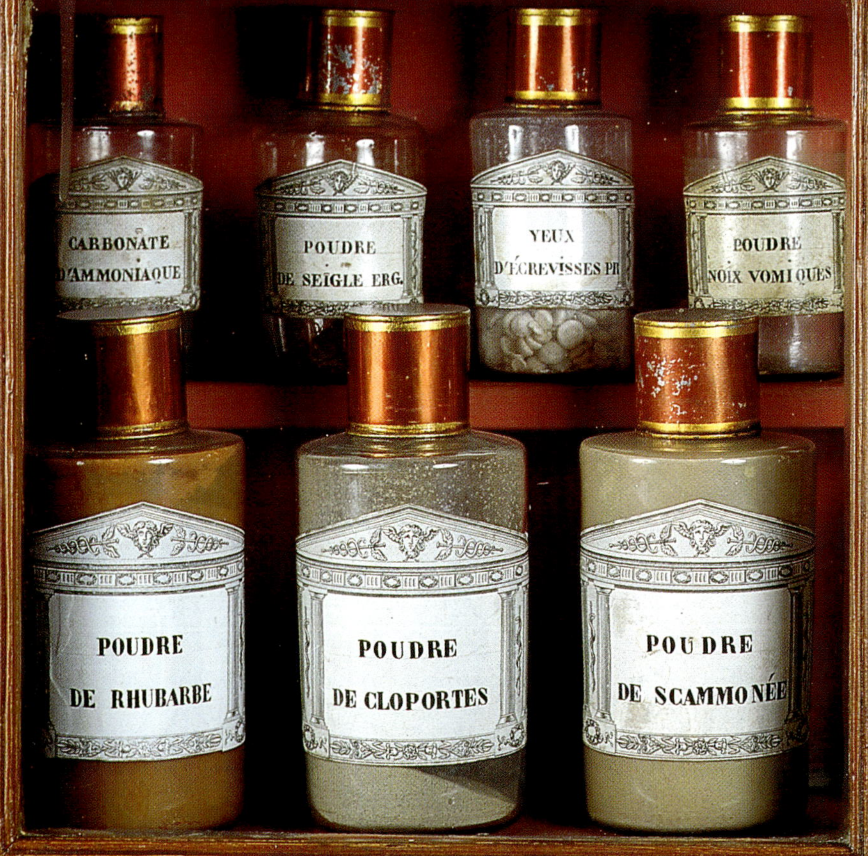

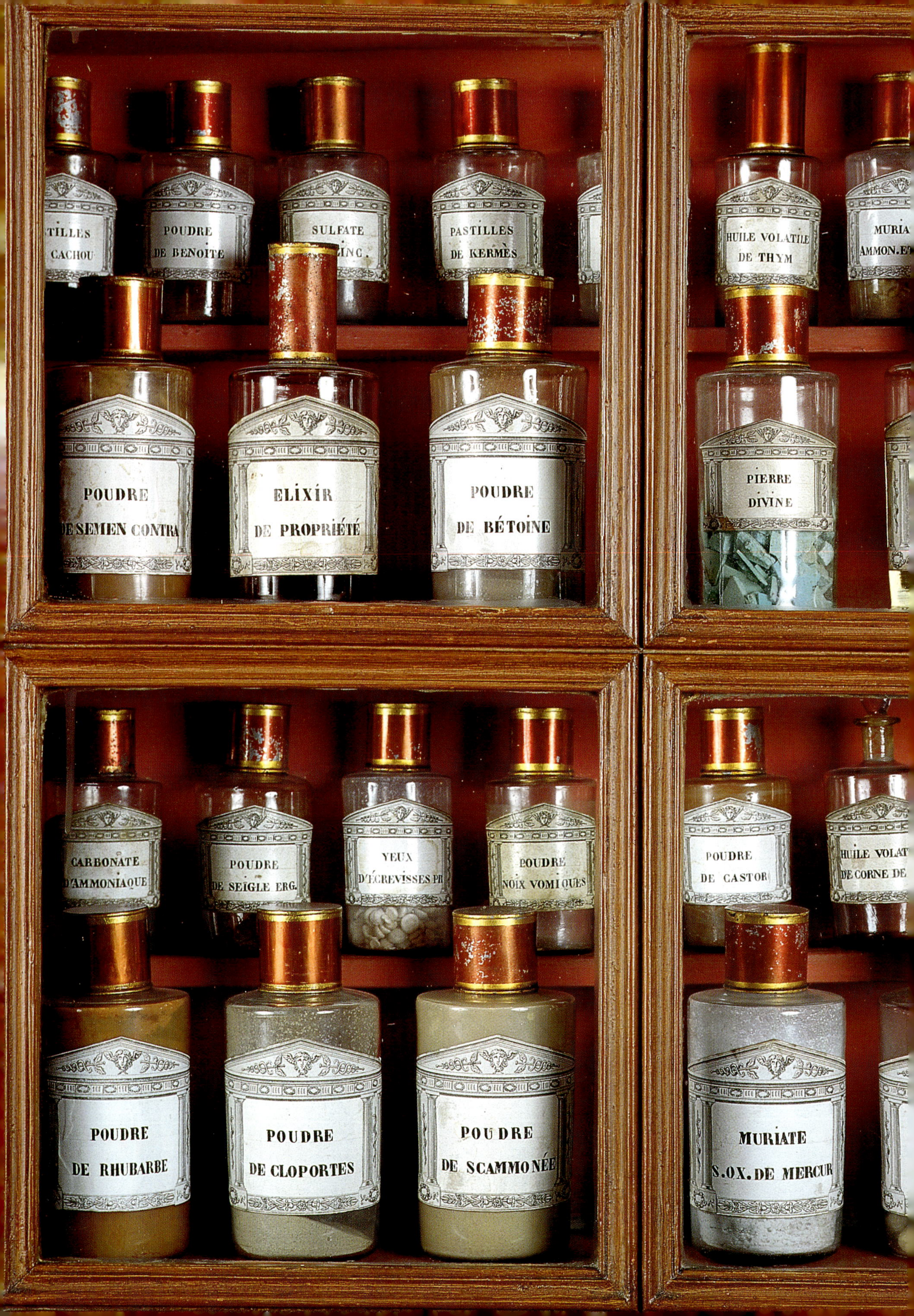
TILLES
CACHOU
POUDRE
DE BENOITE
SULFATE
PASTILLES
DE KERMÈS
HUILE VOLATILE
DE THYM
MURIA
POUDRE
DE SEMEN CONTRA
ELIXIR
DE PROPRIÉTÉ
POUDRE
DE BÉTOINE
PIERRE
DIVINE
CARBONATE
D'AMMONIAQUE
POUDRE
DE SEIGLE ERG.
YEUX
D'ÉCREVISSES PR
POUDRE
NOIX VOMIQUES
POUDRE
DE CASTOR
HUILE VOLAT
DE CORNE DE
POUDRE
DE RHUBARBE
POUDRE
DE CLOPORTES
POUDRE
DE SCAMMONÉE
MURIATE
S.OX. DE MERCUR

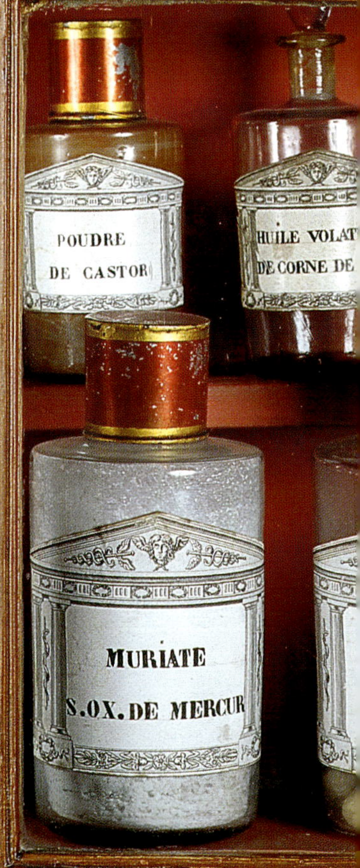

THE HÔTEL-DIEU IN BEAUNE

A palace for the poor

A display cabinet in the pharmacy.

It was in the busy town of Beaune that we visited the most unusual of the châteaux of Burgundy. Beaune is an important crossroads and the capital of the Burgundy wine business. Industrial activity means that the old town is surrounded by modern suburbs, but the surrounding town walls with their fortified towers still protect it. Its prosperity in the Middle Ages came first from the cloth and then from the wine trades, hence the many palatial hôtels, or private mansions, the power of the mayors of Beaune, and the ten religious houses in the town. Its historic sites, however, are not always obvious.

Just like this far from impressive doorway in a rather forbidding wall, which, however, opens out onto another world. As soon as you enter the unevenly paved courtyard, the hum and bustle of the town is left behind. The ornate doors, the long colonnaded gallery, and the roofs of varnished tiles with their two sizes of dormer windows at two different levels transport us into another universe. It is Beaune's Hôtel-Dieu, a palace built for the poor.

Nicolas Rolin, a member of the Autun middle class, worked his way up to be chancellor to Duke Philip the Good of Burgundy. In the 15th century, Burgundy was an independent and prosperous state, which apart from the duchy itself, comprised the county of Burgundy, which was part of the Holy Roman Empire, and included especially the wealthy Low Countries.

Nicolas Rolin, therefore, became extremely rich, like his wife, Guigone de Salins, the heiress of the salt-works near the town of the same name. However, this was a God-fearing period, and to secure a place in paradise, the rich had to help the poor, who acted as intercessors for their salvation. Nicolas and Guigone first had a preference for Autun for the foundation of their hospice, but instead chose Beaune, Burgundy's most important town. It was endowed with the proceeds from the salt-works, on which the duke granted a tax exemption. Both the bodies and souls of the poor and destitute were cared for free of charge in the hospice. The beauty of the place, the splendour of the decoration, and the high quality of the care given to the patients by a community of nuns which had been established in perpetuity, were all worthy of the vast fortune accumulated by Nicolas

LISTE DES VINS ET ALCOOLS OFFERTS

Joseph DROUHIN, à Beaune	*Beaune Clos des Mouches 1955*
Etablissements Louis MAX, à Beaune	*Chassagne-Montrachet 1949*
PATRIARCHE Père & Fils, à Beaune	*Bourgogne blanc « Golden Green » 1952*
Roland THEVENIN, au Château de Puligny-Montrachet et à Saint-Romain	*Puligny-Montrachet Clos de la Garenne 1953*
Léon VIOLLAND, à Beaune	*Savigny-Marconnets blanc 1950*
Albert BICHOT & Cie, à Beaune	*Chambolle-Musigny 1952*
BOUCHARD Aîné & Fils, à Beaune	*Bourgogne Vieilles Vignes 1952*
BOUCHARD Père & Fils, au Château, Beaune	*Beaune Clos de la Mousse 1947*
J. CALVET & Cie, à Beaune	*Clos Vougeot 1949*
Caves du COUVENT DES CORDELIERS, à Beaune	*Beaune 1953*
CHANSON Père & Fils, à Beaune	*Beaune Clos des Marconnets 1953*
G. CORCOL, à Beaune	*Beaune Cent-Vignes 1953*
JAFFELIN Frères, à Beaune	*Beaune Premier Cru 1954*
Louis LATOUR, à Beaune	*Château de Corton-Grancey 1953*
P. DE MARCILLY Frères, à Beaune	*Bourgogne Marcilly Première 1947*
E. & D. MOINGEON Frères, à Beaune	*Chambolle-Musigny 1953*
POULET Père & Fils, à Beaune	*Beaune, Domaine de Saux 1952*
RÉSERVE DES CAVES DE LA ROTISSERIE DE LA REINE PÉDAUQUE, à Beaune	*Savigny-les-Beaune 1952*
Roland THEVENIN, au Château de Puligny-Montrachet et à Saint-Romain	*Musigny 1950* *Saint-Romain 1949*
VERCHERRE & Cie, à Beaune	*Pommard Clos de la Commaraine 1953*
Léon VIOLLAND, à Beaune	*Pommard 1955*
J. LEQUEUX & Cie, à Beaune	*Bourgogne Mousseux blanc*
MOINGEON & REMONDET, à Savigny-les-Beaune	*Bourgogne Mousseux blanc*
Léon VIOLLAND, à Beaune	*Marc des Hospices de Beaune*
E. LABET, à Beaune	*Prunelle de Bourgogne*

Nos hôtes pourront demander à déguster, suivant les disponibilités, un ou plusieurs des grands vins ci-dessus.

AUDITION DES « JOYEUX BOURGUIGNONS »

Le service est assuré par les élèves de 3e année du Collège Technique Hôtelier de Thonon-les-Bains, sous la direction de leurs professeurs.

A block of chocolate with an image of the Hôtel-Dieu.

Dîner de Gala

donné dans
les Grands Celliers des Hospices de Beaune
ce 17 Novembre 1957
au soir de la Vente des Vins.

Rolin. So that neither God nor man should forget him, he also left his cipher everywhere, on the floor tiles that bear the inscription 'seulle' (only), as a reminder of his fidelity to his wife, on the wall-hangings, and on the vertically-woven tapestry bed-covers which were used on feast days. The poor were carefully selected, as the Hôtel-Dieu's charter of 1443, approved by Pope Pius II in a papal bull of 1443, forbade access to those suffering from contagious diseases. In the great 'salle des Pôvres' (hall of the poor), 30 beds accommodated the sick, who each received a copper basin, a spittoon, and a bleeding basin. The air was freshened with perfumes and aromatic herbs, because contaminated air carried sickness, and from their beds, the patients could take part in the church services celebrated in the chapel at the end of the hall. Thus cared for, loved, and comforted, they secured not only their own health, but also that of their benefactors.

Throughout the building, the care given to the smallest detail is amazing. How it must have astounded those admitted here as patients! On top of the altar, that masterpiece of Flemish art, Roger van der Weyden's 'The Last Judgement', used to be opened on high days and holy days. A compassionate Christ watched over this structure standing between heaven and earth. The Hôtel-Dieu outlived its founders. Louis XIV gave money to support it, as did many of the members of the Beaune middle class, who earned the remission of their punishment in purgatory by offering it the vines that bore their name, the produce of which enables the upkeep of a modern hospice.

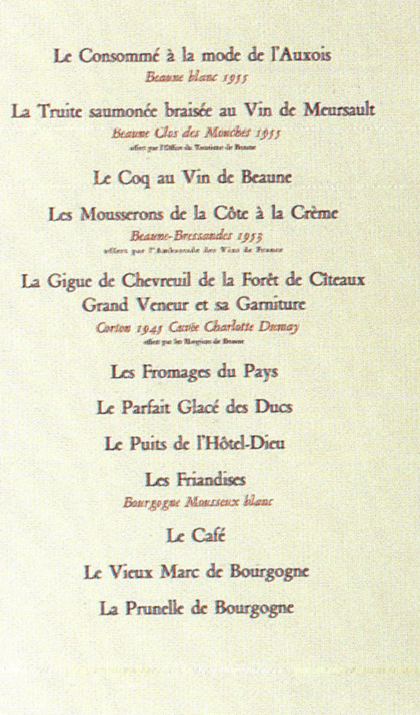

Le Consommé à la mode de l'Auxois
Beaune blanc 1955

La Truite saumonée braisée au Vin de Meursault
Beaune Clos des Mouches 1955
offert par l'Office du Tourisme de Beaune

Le Coq au Vin de Beaune

Les Mousserons de la Côte à la Crème
Beaune-Bressandes 1953
offert par l'Ambassade des Vins de France

La Gigue de Chevreuil de la Forêt de Cîteaux
Grand Veneur et sa Garniture
Corton 1945 Cuvée Charlotte Dumay

Les Fromages du Pays

Le Parfait Glacé des Ducs

Le Puits de l'Hôtel-Dieu

Les Friandises
Bourgogne Mousseux blanc

Le Café

Le Vieux Marc de Bourgogne

La Prunelle de Bourgogne

'This hospital makes you want to fall ill in Beaune'
(Viollet-le-Duc).

The medical kitchen at the Hôtel-Dieu contains preparations of proved efficaciousness, of medicinal herbs and many other different ingredients, which were ground in a mortar, e.g.:

– medicinal spirits of mint, roses, lemon balm, lemon, or Assa foetida,

– acids, ethers, opiates for pain, digitalis for the heart, rhubarb for the digestion, and stag horn,

– powders of beaver, wood-louse, feverfew, aloe, madder, pansies, arnica, and cuttlebone,

– pastilles of marsh-mallow, burnt sponge, powdered rye… or the eyes of freshwater crayfish !

Symbolism and empiricism were the two foundations of this pharmacopoeia. For the most difficult cases, about fifty ingredients would be ground up, a little opium would be added, and then prayers said. Surgery was also carried out, the surgical instruments being kept today in one of the other rooms. In 1788, it was here that a woman was authorised to work as a pharmacist for the first time.

Healthy diet for plague victims

'Meat will be seasoned. Salads with sharp-tasting sauces, like those containing the juice of pomegranates, oranges, and lemons, that lance the large 'humours', and gruel will be cooked with blood-purifying herbs, such as borage, bugloss, chicory, marigold, pimpernel, hyssop, marjoram, and purslane.

At the same time, genuine, unrefined essence of anise should be tried, the patient taking seven or eight drops in winter mixed with a spoonful of good wine and mixed with some fruit cordials. It goes without saying that raw fruits and poor quality meat are absolutely forbidden. Drinks are to be beer, light red wine, or herbal tea'.

(extract from a Dijon doctors' manual of 1557).

Meat broth.

Chicken wine

Mix an egg yolk with some sugar until the mixture turns white, then pour in some hot red wine. Effective against tiredness and feeling cold.

Fortifying and healthy meat broth

'When the condition of the convalescing patient does not enable him to immediately stomach as strong a consommé as usual, a healthy meat broth should be prepared for him in the following way, in order to help him towards a more substantial diet.

In a cooking-pot, put 4 litres of water, 1500g of sliced beef, a chicken, and 1 kilo of shin of veal. When you have skimmed the broth, add 4 carrots, as well as some large onions, a large, firm lettuce, and a handful of chervil. When the broth is ready and has been strained, it can be served as it is, or else as a base for the making of soups with vermicelli, rice, or tapioca.'

Wrinkle cream

'Crush white lily bulbs in a marble mortar, and squeeze out the juice. Melt 60g of white wax over a very low heat. Pour the molten wax into a marble mortar, which has been pre-warmed by pouring some boiling water into it, so that the molten wax does not set immediately. Into the molten wax, mix 60g of white lily juice and 60g of the finest Narbonne honey, stirring briskly for a long time. Add some drops of bergamot essence. Spread this cream over the face at night before sleeping, and remove it in the morning by washing with a very light soap and water. This cosmetic is ineffective against creases in the skin that are not really wrinkles caused by age, but which are the result of frequent frowning, due to habitual irritability and bad temper, against which no cream can ever be effective.'

The Hôtel-Dieu is not only a museum, as the nursing nuns are still there, and a hospital stands adjacent to the old buildings. The nuns' kitchen, now little used, has been replaced by a modern kitchen, where Monsieur Vernet, the head chef, who has given us some of his recipes, devotes himself to the preparation of delicious meals.

The mechanically-powered Messire Bertrand is a celebrity, as he has turned the spit in the great fireplace ever since 1698.

BURGUNDY BEEF

Marinade some pieces of beef taken from the shoulder (which is more gelatinous) or shin, together with a 'garniture aromatique' (bouquet garni, onions, and carrots) in a full-bodied red Burgundy wine.
Leave to marinade overnight.
Brown thoroughly the drained pieces of meat in oil. Skim off the fat and then sprinkle them with flour. Add the marinade, the bouquet garni, carrots, and onions, and cook on a low heat for 2 hours.
During the cooking time, glaze until brown some small, round onions, button mushrooms, and smoky bacon, i.e. cook them in just enough water to cover them with some butter, sprinkle with caster sugar, and cover with tin-foil, until the water boils away. Stir from time to time to ensure an even glazing.
Mix this with the 'boeuf bourguignon'. Check the thickness of the sauce, and, if necessary, add some 'beurre manié' (butter and flour).

The river Bouzaize flows under the kitchen. The great double fireplace was used for cooking for the sick for over five hundred years.

A real 'boeuf bourguignon', standing here on the 19th century cast-iron oven.

The cooking can also be finished in the oven, in a covered casserole, or even better coated with flour.
And what should be drunk with it? You could choose a country wine like a Grand Ordinaire Burgundy, or else a good Rully or a full-bodied Pommard.

HAM IN A WINE LEES SAUCE

This is ham cooked in the wine lees (dregs), a thick and purplish-blue liquid, that are left after the grape pressing. The ham will be put to marinade in the wine lees with a 'garniture aromatique' (some carrots and onions, and a bouquet garni) over two nights.
Prepare a stock with onion, carrot, thyme, bay, and parsley, and cook the ham in it. It should not be allowed to boil as that makes the meat tough. Cook for 3 hours.
Drain the ham, bone it, and put it in an oven dish to braise it. Add the wine lees and the 'garniture aromatique'. The meat should be well-browned. Baste the ham with the wine lees at frequent intervals.
When cooked, reduce the sauce, and thicken with some 'beurre manié'.
Prepare some vegetables 'grand-mère' by glazing some small onions and mushrooms, and some diced bacon, and add to the sauce.

PORK FILLET WITH A MUSTARD SAUCE

Take a pork fillet, remove the tendons, and cook it whole. To stay tender, a 'filet mignon' (small fillet steak) should not be cooked long, about 1/2 hour is enough.
Remove the fat and deglaze with some white wine. Add some veal stock and double cream, season, leave to reduce a little, and when cooked, add some mustard grains.
Accompany this with a red wine that is not too tannic, or with a white Chardonnay.

CHICKEN IN A CHAMBERTIN SAUCE

Dress and singe a good-sized chicken, and cut it into about ten pieces.
Reserve the liver and blood for thickening the sauce.
Make a marinade with a

bottle of Chambertin, a small glass of cognac, a spoonful of olive oil, two sliced large carrots, three peeled and finely sliced large onions, some unpeeled cloves of garlic, and a bouquet garni. Add the chicken, mix well, and leave to marinade for about twelve hours.
At the end of the marinading time, drain the chicken pieces, and brown them in olive oil. Add the vegetables from the marinade and sprinkle flour over it all. Stir and leave to brown a bit.
Pour in the wine from the marinade and a quarter litre of either veal or chicken stock.
Add some more Chambertin wine until the chicken is just covered. Cook for about an hour over a low heat.
Meanwhile, prepare some glazed small round onions, some mushrooms, and some diced bacon, and add these to the dish.
When cooked, arrange the chicken pieces on a dish, and keep warm. Strain the sauce through a conical sieve, and remove the fat, if necessary. Chop the liver, mix with the blood, and thicken the sauce with it.
If that does not appeal to you, thicken the sauce with some 'beurre manié'. Cover the dish with the sauce, and scatter the glazed onions, mushrooms, and diced bacon over it.
Fried croûtons and potatoes 'à l'anglaise' (boiled potatoes) go well with the 'coq au Chambertin'.
It is advisable for the Chambertin to be kept for the recipe and not for drinking, when it should be replaced by a full-bodied, but less distinguished, wine.

BLACKCURRANT TART

For the pastry case:
250 g flour,
125 g butter,
1 egg yolk,
50 g sugar,
a pinch of salt, and
5 cl water.
Mix together, roll out, and leave to rest for an hour.
Put your pastry in a buttered tart tin, and scatter it with blackcurrants.
For the filling, mix 40 cl milk, 40 cl 'crème fraîche' (slightly soured cream), and three eggs beaten with 100 g caster sugar. Flavour with a little vanilla essence.
Pour onto the blackcurrants, and cook for not more than 30 minutes, first of all for 10 minutes at 250°C, and then at 20 minutes at 200°C.
Sprinkle with icing sugar before serving, preferably hot.

ALMOND AND BLACKCURRANT TART

Make the pastry for the tart using the previous recipe. The pastry should be cooked blind for about 20 minutes (cover the base with some dried beans to prevent it from rising). The 'amandine' mixture is made from 100 g butter, 100 g sugar, 100 g ground almonds, and two eggs. Mix it all together, put it into the pastry case (having first taken out the dried beans), and cover with a pound of blackcurrants. Bake in the oven for about 15 minutes. Serve hot or cold, sprinkled with some icing sugar.

PEAR IN SPICED RED WINE, WITH ICE-CREAM AND CRÈME DE CASSIS

Peel the pears (one for each person), leaving the stem on. Heat 1/2 litre of a red Burgundy with some spices, e.g. cloves, cinnamon, and orange peel, 20 cl water, and 300 g sugar. Put the pears into the simmering liquid and cook for about 30 minutes.
Check to see whether the pears are cooked by pricking the centres with a needle.
Remove the pears carefully, and boil the liquid until it has a thick, syrupy consistency.
Put some vanilla ice-cream and the pear covered in syrup into some small bowls, adding a little crème de cassis. Decorate, if you like, with toasted almonds or 'crème Chantilly'.

When admitted to the Hôtel-Dieu, each patient received a set of essential utensils, made of pewter.

A Burgundian Fanfare

Burgundy is certainly a great and beautiful region, with an abundance of places of interest, history, and historic buildings. But the wines of Burgundy… ah!

To Burgundy belong the forests and hills, the fields of the Yonne with their chalky outcrops, the rich pastures of Charolais, the wetlands of Bresse, the châteaux, whether magnificent or more intimate in scale, and the many colours of the different roofing materials of tiles, lava, or slates. To Burgundy belong the hillsides of gold and purple, with the many scattered vineyards and the wine-producing villages with their narrow winding streets, the two colours washing together into a single chart of gorgeous colours.

The officially registered Burgundy vineyards only occupy a hundredth of the region, but they form its jewel in the crown. A narrow band of poor soil runs between the plain and the uplands from Dijon to Mâcon, and on it are situated towns and villages whose very names make wine-lovers the world over drool. There is Gevrey, with its strong deep red wines; Morey, vigorous and long-keeping; Chamolle, delicate; Vougeot, full-bodied and velvety, with the scent of violets; Vosne, superbly elegant; Nuits, both well-rounded and full-bodied; Aloxe, inscrutable and classy in both red and white; Beaune, pleasant and graceful; Pommard, robust and enduring; Volnay, subtle and of excellent stock; Meursault, white wines with the taste of butter and hazelnut; Puligny and Chassagne, noble and flowery, and many, many others.

It was the monks that first planted vines around these villages, whose houses were built by the wine growers. Their names have often become hyphenated with the addition of the name of their finest vineyard, e.g. Gevrey-Chambertin, Nuits-Saint-Georges, Vosne-Romanée, Aloxe-Corton, Puligny-Montrachet, a real case of the conferment of noble status upon the successful execution of duties.

Burgundy wines have need of headings. Firstly, there is a kind of Debrett's Peerage for the wines of special quality, the 'grand' and 'premiers' crus'. There must also be family histories, detailing disputes, both ancient and modern. There must also be the châteaux, with their walled vineyards, their gates, and the gateways bearing their name. We photographed several of these during our trip around the vineyards.

Festivities are also essential, and here, Burgundy never lags behind. There are wine festivals every year on St Vincent's day (September 27), when the villages welcome each other to the many celebrations and gatherings. The most important of these is the 'Trois Glorieuses', which takes place on the third Saturday in November, when an assembly of the Confrérie des Chevaliers du Tastevin is held at the château of Clos de Vougeot. The following day, the most celebrated auction in the

world, the famous sale of barrelled wine at the Hospices de Beaune, takes place. On the Monday is the Paulée de Meursault, which is a real Burgundian banquet at which bottles of the best wine are swapped around from table to table. However, like all noble families, Burgundy has also suffered death on the battlefield, but here it has been because of phylloxera, or money, or changing fashions, that the great names have not been able to stand firm. Who now remembers Côte d'Auxerre, Chaînette, Vaumorillon, or Olivottes, names that almost 200 years ago were considered to be among the very best wines in France? As for the vineyard of the Dukes of Burgundy at Chenove, that has been swallowed up by the expansion of Dijon's built-up area.

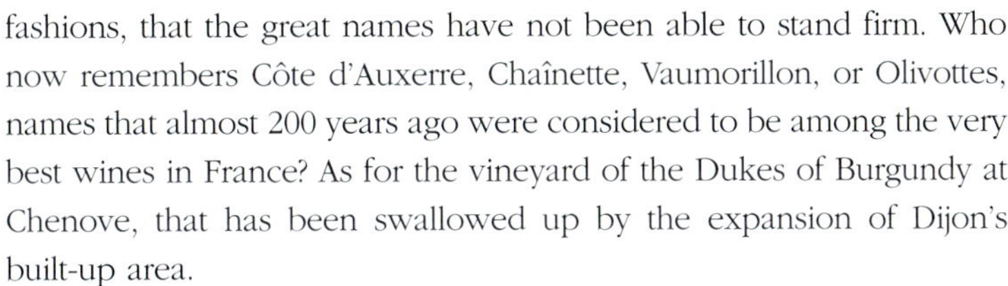

Fortunately, some of the old vineyards have come back to life again. The hillsides at Vézelay have been replanted, and white and sparkling wines have successfully reappeared at Tonnerre. To hail this revival, here are two recipes based on good Burgundy wine, which were given to us by our aunt, Thérèse d'Origny, who welcomed us to the town of Origny, under which flows a mysterious underground spring.

Aunt Thérèse's gougères

50 cl milk, 5 g salt, 125 g butter. Bring these ingredients to the boil. Remove from the heat and add 250 g of flour. Stir for a minute over the heat to dry out the pastry. Remove from the heat, and add eight eggs, two by two, followed by 125 g of diced gruyere. Put into a greased ring-shaped baking tin or in small heaps onto a greased baking sheet. Bake in a hot oven.

Veal in a red wine sauce

Brown some pieces of topside or chump end of veal. Sprinkle with flour, and cook over a low heat for 1 minute. Add some red Burgundy until the meat is just covered. Stir well, and cook over a very low heat for a good hour. Season before serving. Simple and good.

What should be served with it? Why not a Savigny-les Beaune?

VÉZELAY

The eternal hill

'Cabalus' apple tart, as enjoyed at the Hôtellerie de Vézelay.

The Burgundian always seems to have his feet planted firmly on the ground in this land of broad hilltops that are so voluptuous in the Yonne, and so bountiful everywhere. But there is also a spiritual dimension to Burgundy, as it provided the solid foundation for Romanesque architecture at Cluny and Cîteaux, later had leanings for the Gothic style, has many cathedrals and churches, and, of course, Vézelay.

The inscription - and the cannonballs - commemorate the siege of Vézelay in 1569 during the Wars of Religion.

Admittedly, it is not a château, but we simply had to include it in this book. Vézelay, the eternal hill, is more than just an historic monument, it is a gateway through which kings, pilgrims, and poets have passed for over a thousand years. Proust, Eluard, Claudel, Picasso, and many others came to Vézelay, and Max-Pol Fouchet, Clavel, and Bataille are buried there. Every evening, when the flood of tourists to this Mont-Saint-Michel on dry land has abated, you tell yourself that you could stay on this rock, which is rather like an island after the departure of the last boat, a long time, without ever tiring of it. And then you leave it again, like so many others do, but heartened by your secret vow.

Vézelay's glory only lasted for a few centuries – those of the worship of St Mary Magdalene, who was the first witness of Christ's resurrection – but its influence was exceptionally important. The monastery was placed under the direct control of the Pope in the 9th century, but was then freed from papal control by King Louis the Fat. This privileged status was the cause of constant battles for power between the Counts of Nevers, the bishops of Autun, Cluny Abbey, and even the middle-class citizens of Vézelay, which was by then an important town. The relics of St Mary Magdalene, which had been removed from Arles and declared authentic by the Pope, made Vézelay an important place of pilgrimage. The church was destroyed by fire in 970, was subsequently reconstructed, but burned down again on the Day of Atonement, 22 July, 1120,

The Hôtellerie was built at the same time as the abbey, and has shared both the good and the bad times.

A fresco depicting the arrival of pilgrims at a church (from Brancion in Burgundy). From the book 'Les chemins de Compostelle en terre de France' (The roads to Compostella in France), published by Editions Ouest-France.

causing 1,000 deaths, and was reconstructed yet again. Each time, new pilgrims climbed up the hill.

In 1146, they were called King Louis and Queen Eleanor of France, and Duke Eudes of Burgundy. St Bernard preached the Crusades there. Crosses were given out to the volunteers, and then fabric crosses cut out of cloth. More than 100,000 men, both French and Germanic, set off the following year, only to be defeated and their king taken prisoner.

In 1190, they were called Richard the Lionheart and Philip Augustus. More than 15,000 men, French, Germanic, and English, set out on the Third Crusade.

However, between the comings and goings of men-at-arms, and between the two disputes between the abbot of Vézelay and the Count of Nevers, the abbey was witness to the tightly-packed rows of pilgrims to Santiago de Compostella climbing upwards through the vineyards, as Vézelay was the departure point for the Via Lemovicensis, the Limoges Way, which was one of the four great

The vaulted 12th century hall has seen St Bernard and King Louis VII pass by. Bread is still baked in the oven here, and in the cooking-pot, there is always a constant supply of delicious hot soup for the guests of the 'eternal hill'.

routes of the most important pilgrimage in Europe. They assembled here, stayed at the inn with a cockle shell above its doorway, and then set off on their journey through the Morvan forests.

From the 13th century onwards, Vézelay's glory began to fade. Of course, St Louis paid four visits, and a Franciscan monastery was established. But the major routes gradually moved away, and the cult of St Mary Magdalene moved to Provence.

The abbey could no longer afford the upkeep of its property, and in 1538, Vézelay was secularised. It was no longer the monks, but the ordinary clergy that administered it, along with the commendatory, or lay, abbots, who attached more importance to their revenues than to the enlightenment of souls. The first of these abbots was Odet de Coligny, the brother of the famous admiral. This curious character

became a Calvinist and was excommunicated by Pope Pious IV, but nevertheless got married in his cardinal's robes.

However, the death throes of Vézelay had not yet come to an end, as the exquisitely beautiful tympanum was damaged by hammer blows, and the monastery buildings were destroyed during the Revolution.

In 1834, Prosper Mérimée, the author and inspector of historical monuments, could not fail to notice the extremely dilapidated state of the buildings, which had been stricken yet again by another fire. The young architect, Viollet-le-Duc was put in charge of the restoration work, and was successful in giving back to the abbey, now a church, all of its beauty and mystery.

In 1876, the relics of St Mary Magdalene returned to Vézelay, and ever since, the bustle of visitors has never ceased. Just as they did 1,000 years before, they climb up the village's two streets, or cross the recently replanted vineyard. Just as they did 1,000 years before, they stop at the inn to have something to eat before leaving – each one going his own way.

We, like them, also stopped at this inn, and have brought you a few souvenirs back.

An 'hôtellerie', or inn, feeds both the body and the spirit, providing simple, healthy food, a homely atmosphere, and clean rooms with a well-filled library. But the gift of languages is recommended, as well as some pictures, such as these engravings belonging to the mistress of the establishment.

At the entrance to the Hôtellerie can be seen the pilgrims' scallop shell, which acted as a waymark for the many stages of the pilgrimage route to Santiago de Compostella.

PILGRIM'S SOUP

This soup is made in a large cooking-pot on a low heat.
Trim the ends and green tops off some leeks. Cut the leeks in four from top to bottom without cutting down to the end. Clean them under running water to wash away any soil.
Peel some carrots, trimming off the ends.
Peel some onions and some potatoes. Wash some courgettes, and, if very big, peel off the skin.
Take off the stalks of some tomatoes.
Finely slice the leeks, carrots, and onions.
Cut the potatoes into small pieces, dice the courgettes, and cut the tomatoes into four.
Put all the vegetables into the cooking-pot and barely cover with water.
Throw in a large handful of coarse salt.
After bringing to the boil, cook gently until all the vegetables are blended together. Pour through a wide-meshed sieve or vegetable mill. Serve in a bowl, eating with a slice of bread baked in a wood-fired stove.

'CABALUS' APPLE PUFF PASTRY TART

Make some flaky pastry with 300 g flour (plus 50 g for the working of the pastry),
250 g butter,
6 g table salt, dissolved in 15 cl water.
Put the flour onto a marble surface, make a well in the centre, and pour in the cold water and salt.
Knead the flour and water with the fingertips so that all the water is absorbed, but take care not to overdo this.
Add a little more water if needed.
Next, make the pastry into a smooth and fairly soft ball.
Roll out the pastry with a rolling pin on the floured marble surface. The centre should be thicker than the edges.
Put some butter of the same consistency as the pastry in the middle of it.
Cover the butter completely by bringing the edges of the pastry towards the centre.
Give the pastry a few taps with the rolling pin so as to spread out the butter, and to give it a square shape.
Roll out a rectangle 1 or 2 cm thick. Even out the edges with the rolling pin.
Fold 1/3 of the pastry into the centre, then the other third over that.

Give the pastry a half turn.
The fold should now be to the left and right of you.
Repeat the whole process.
Roll out to the same size, fold into three parts,
Mark the pastry with two light fingerprints to show that it has been turned twice.
Now rest the pastry for 10 minutes in a cool place.
Repeat the whole process for the third and fourth turns, keeping the marble surface well-floured.
Place the fold to the left and right.
Mark the pastry with four fingerprints, rest it in a cool place for a further 10 minutes.
Repeat the process for the fifth and sixth turns (flour the marble surface well, have the fold running from left to right, roll out, and follow the same process as previously).
The flaky pastry is now ready, but another method is simply to order a flaky pastry case from your baker!
Spread the pastry into a greased tart tin.
Peel a good pound of undamaged apples, slice thinly, and arrange them decoratively on the pastry.
Mix three eggs with 40 cl double cream (or if need be, a little milk), and 100 g brown sugar.
Pour this over the apples and bake in a hot oven for about 30 minutes.
Keep careful watch while the tart is cooking.

*B*OURBILLY

A château in the countryside

The château's private kitchen, which is entered through a Gothic arch from the former keep.

At Bourbilly, Baron Edouard de Crépy himself cooked the 'rapée morvandelle' and 'saupiquet de jambon' for us. The kitchen is always a warm and lively place in this family home in which children and grandchildren come to stay throughout the summer. The château is only gradually being modernised, but then a château is never finished, and when you live in one, there is no end of improvement work to be done.

Through the Bourbilly estate flows the river Serein, which then continues on its way through the vineyards of Chablis and along the edge of the Auxois plain, before reaching the wooded foothills of the Morvan. Bourbilly's name undoubtedly comes from its situation, which used to be a 'bourbier' or marsh that was frequently flooded. The park is now well-drained, and the water here is now under control, mainly in the form of the mirror-like surfaces of three granite lakes. The tennis court is one of the oldest in France, and is still marked out in the old measurements.

The estate used to be part of the royal domaine, then passed, in 1032, to the dukes of Burgundy, and then, in 1189, to André of Montbard. The château was built in the 14th century by Marguerite de Baujeu, whose son, Louis of Savoy, sold Bourbilly to the La Trémoïlle family. At the peak of the duchy of Burgundy's power, Bourbilly finally passed into the ownership of the Montagu family, and, by marriage, to the Rabutins. In 1592, the marriage of Christophe de Rabutin, Baron

The château can only be fully appreciated by walking round it. It used to be fortified, but was gradually opened up, and a lot of damage was caused during the Revolution. Major reconstruction works during the 19th century gave it its present appearance, whereby the different styles of the various facades blend together to give the château a single soul. The lofty chimneys are called the 'demoiselles', and were the first covered chimneys in France.

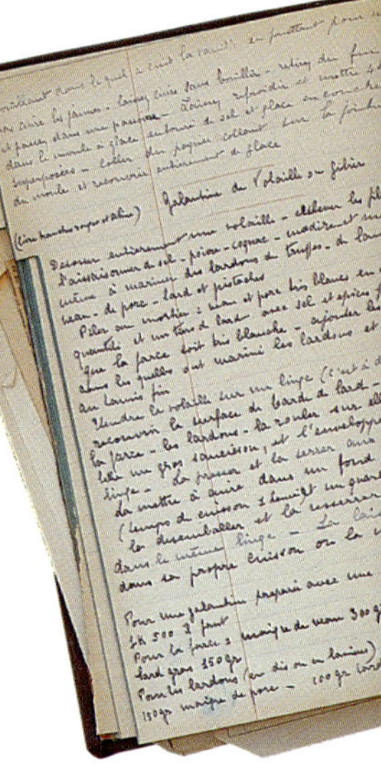

The family's large, well-filled recipe books. Each generation has used and added to them.

The battery of copper pots and pans in the kitchen, together with the servants' lockers. Bourbilly was a large household, and employed twelve people in the pantries and kitchens.

de Chantal, to Jeanne Frémiot, daughter of the president of the Burgundy parliament, was celebrated in the chapel at Bourbilly. They had six children, including Celse-Bénigne, Madame de Sévigné's father.

After her husband's accidental death in 1601, Jeanne de Chantal went to live near Autun, where she got to know François de Sales, the then bishop of Annecy. Under his authority, she founded the religious order of the Visitandines, which today has 160 monasteries. Canonised in 1767, St Jeanne de Chantal is the patron saint of Burgundy. Her chapel at

A coffee grinder.

Bourbilly, which is also the parish church, formed part of the lives of future owners of the château up to the marriage on 7 April, 1952, of Chantal Darcy, whose family had owned the château since 1813, and Baron Edouard de Crépy. Unfortunately, the chapel was completely destroyed in a fire three months later. The reconstruction work lasted for fifteen years, at great cost both in determination and in financial sacrifice on the part on the whole family.

Bourbilly holds other treasures, such as the living room that was built in the 19th century on the site of the old drawbridge. The inherited wealth of Mme de Crépy's great-grandfather, Charles de Franqueville, the maker of Erard pianos enabled important work to be done to the house. De Franqueville had nine superb glass chandeliers made at Murano. These are made up of 6,000 pieces of glass, all of which must be cleaned with infini-

These 'petits pots à crème' are an absolutely essential part of the equipment needed for the making of desserts.

The dining room can accommodate forty people at the same time. Within its thick walls, the décor and furnishings are Gothic in inspiration.

te care with a toothbrush. These chandeliers have seen lighting by candle, by acetylene, by generator-produced electricity, and by mains electricity since 1952 ... with 110 volts. Life in a château does also have its limitations.

HAM IN A PIQUANT RED WINE AND VINEGAR SAUCE

Carve some slices from a ham on the bone. Reduce some chopped shallots in a little wine and stock, then add a little vinegar, some juniper berries, salt, and pepper. Make a roux of half flour and half butter, and mix with some white wine and a little stock. Add the reduced wine and shallots mixture. Simmer. Sauté the ham slices in butter until well-browned, sieve the sauce, and pour over the ham. Serve with a purée of celery with cream.

GRATED POTATO PANCAKE, WITH CREAM, EGGS AND CHEESE

For 6 people:
500 g potatoes,
10 g butter, 3 eggs,
60 g grated Gruyère,
60 g flour, 10 cl water.
Boil the water and butter.
Remove from the heat, add the flour, and stir well until smooth.
Add the Gruyère.
Roll the mixture into a ball, and leave to cool.
Add the eggs, salt, pepper ('fromage blanc' as an optional extra), and the roughly grated potatoes, dried in a tea-cloth to remove as much starch as possible.
Drop spoonfuls of the mixture into very hot oil, keeping them well separated. Fry for 5 minutes, then take out.
Before serving them very hot, put them back into the hot oil for 2 minutes.
Drain and serve with a salad.

SPINACH PANCAKES

Make a dozen small savoury pancakes with a batter of:
1/2 lb flour,
3 eggs,
1 spoonful brandy,
1 spoonful olive oil,
a pinch of salt,
mixed with a little water and the same quantity of milk.
Leave to rest for 3 hours.
Cook the pancakes in the pan as normal.

Traditional 'râpée morvandelle' (grated potato pancake, with cream, eggs, and cheese): both tasty and attractive.

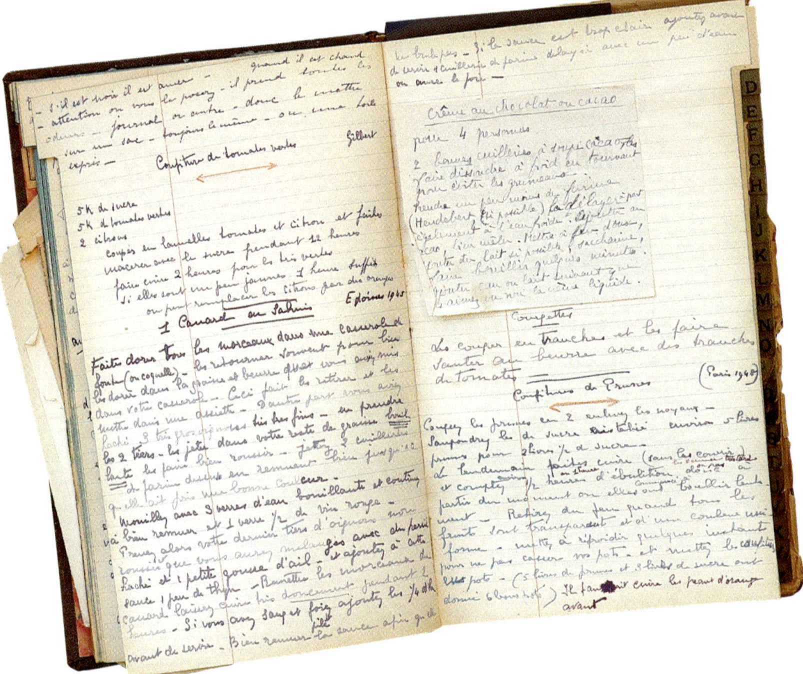

Make the pancake filling:
1 lb of blanched and chopped spinach sautéed in butter, with a little cheese sauce added, and
120 g of coarsely chopped mushrooms, sautéed in butter.
Put a little of the filling on each pancake, then roll it up, putting it on a greased plate for baking in the oven.
Put a little butter and grated cheese on the pancakes, and brown for a few minutes in a hot oven.
Serve very hot.

PHEASANT COOKED IN ITS OWN JUICES

'Clean the pheasant and put a few rashers of fat bacon inside it. Cover its back with another rasher of fat bacon.
Brown the pheasant in a little butter in a casserole dish, add a little water, and cover.
From 11am to 12 noon: cook over a low heat.
Halfway through the cooking, add some thyme, some bay leaves, and some salt and pepper.
Preheat your oven.
At 12 noon: place uncovered in the oven, basting well.
At 12.15 pm: cover the casserole to prevent the pheasant drying out.
At 12.30 pm : serve the pheasant with some fried croûtons and the meat juices.
Serve the rest of the pheasant juices in a gravy boat.
Pheasants cooked in this way will not go dry.'
This is a really handy recipe.
Good cooking also involves good timing.
And what should go with it?
A good fine wine, such as a Vosne or Chambolle.

BOURBILLY LIGHT FRUIT CAKE

For 2 small or 1 very large cake:
140 g butter,
250 g flour,
300 g raisins and candied orange peel
(see the following recipe),
90 g sugar, 3 eggs,
and a packet of baking powder. Soften the butter.
Mix the eggs and sugar

together, and add the butter. Sieve the flour and baking powder together into the mixture. Add the raisins and the candied orange peel.

Stir the cake mixture well, grease a cake tin, and pour it in. Bake in a medium oven, inserting the point of a knife into the cake to check whether it is cooked.

CANDIED ORANGE PEEL

This is an excellent recipe. Blanch pieces of orange peel by putting them into some boiling water (on a corner of the stove) for 8 hours. The water should be changed 3 or 4 times, and the peel should be allowed quite a long time to drain, before being then cooked in a sugar syrup. Allow the syrup to reduce until it thickens. A pound of sugar should generally be allowed for every pound of orange peel.
Cover the casserole during the cooking of the syrup and the peel.

ABOUT THE BOURBILLETTE AND SEVERAL OTHER LOCAL FEATURES

Lying on the borders of Auxois and the rugged region of the Morvan, Bourbilly appears to be a very romantic place to live. However, there are still traces in the château's foundations of a much more forbidding fortress, as described in an inventory of 1796:
'From the outside, it is formed of four sides of different size, in which there are very few openings, and not even any at all in the south-western wall.'
In the shelter of the surrounding wall lay the farmyard, the vegetable garden, the dovecote, and the communal oven. Bourbilly was more than a château. It was the centre of a community who took refuge there in times of trouble – of which there were many. There were vineyards, which have long disappeared, and two mills, the last of which stopped working in 1918, after 600 years of activity. There were ponds, and a well that was replaced in 1907 by water piped in from a spring called the 'Bourbillotte'.
The château that we see today has little in common with that described in 1673 by the Marquise de Sévigné: 'I have now arrived at the château of my forefathers. Here is where they triumphed following the fashion of the time. I have found my beautiful meadows, my magnificent woods, and my fine mill, in the same places as I had left them.'
But from all these layers of history has emerged charm and serenity. Bourbilly is a delightful country château.

Serried ranks of wine glasses in a cupboard in the pantry.

Commarin

The rooftop of the western world

The private dining room at Commarin. It should have been moved into a room in another wing in 1805, but this was occupied by an elderly servant of the château… who lived there until he died at the age of 99.

In the area immortalised by Henri Vincent, a local boy and writer, who was always passionately fond of Burgundy and of its villages, especially Commarin, which he called 'the rooftop of the western world' because its rivers and streams flow into the rivers Saône, Loire, and Seine, a far from commonplace occurrence, we stopped at the château of Commarin, which seems like an oasis of tranquillity in old Burgundy.

The archives of the château of Commarin, which go back to the 14th century, are those of a house which has never been sold nor abandoned. This fact is rare enough in France to help to explain the air of assurance pervading the château, where the celebrated tapestries take the place of a family tree. Each of the family treasures amassed here is a souvenir of a particular period or ancestor.

To a fortified manor house recorded in the 14th century, Commarin added a chapel and some defensive towers, seen by King François I, and then the de Vienne family took over from the Dinteville family, as well as all those other families of whose names no record remains. The tapestries woven for the marriage of Girard de Vienne, a royal knight, and Bénigne de Dinteville in 1500 are, like the even older ones from the time of the marriage of Jacques de Dinteville and Alix de Pontallier, masterpieces of composition and colour, whose heraldic intricacy and excellent state of preservation are awe-inspiring.

Commarin's account books are witnesses of another age and invaluable source material for the historian.

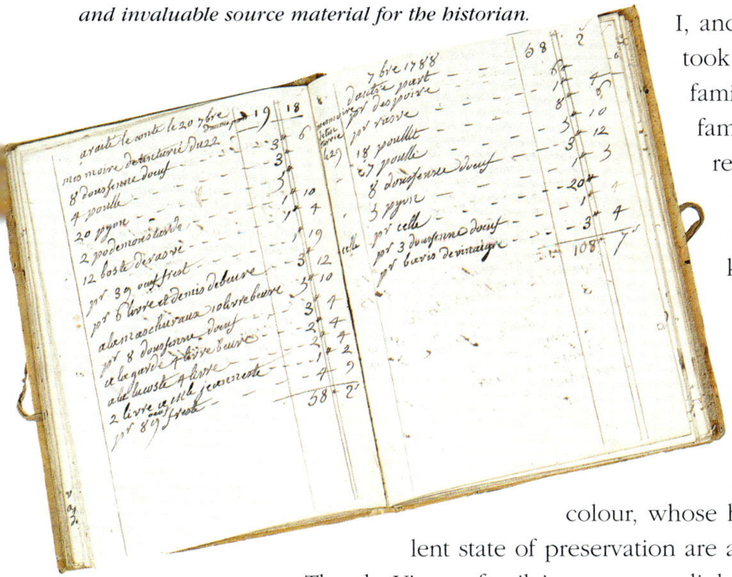

The de Vienne family's name was linked to that of Commarin for two hundred years. In 1698, Charles II de Vienne married Anne de Chastellux, a member of an important Burgundian family. The marriage took place in the Morvan at the château of Chastellux, which had belonged to the family since the 11th century. In 1702, at the age of 3, their daughter, Marie-Judith, laid the first stone of the classical-style facade that can still be admired at Commarin today, and who was to be a major influence in the life of the château until 1780. She married the Marquis of Damas, but was widowed young, and brought up her two children while ceaselessly building stables, outbuildings, and flower beds at Commarin. She ensured that her children married well, a Talleyrand for Alexandrine, and a Rochechouart for Jacques.

Commarin's account books reflect 18th century life in a large country house, rich, to be sure, but with no financial help from outside. Entries on jobs, wages, and payments in kind give us precious information on the life of the aristocracy and the household staff.

'Louis, a cook, entered our service on 26 October, 1699, and I have promised him seventy-five pounds in wages.'

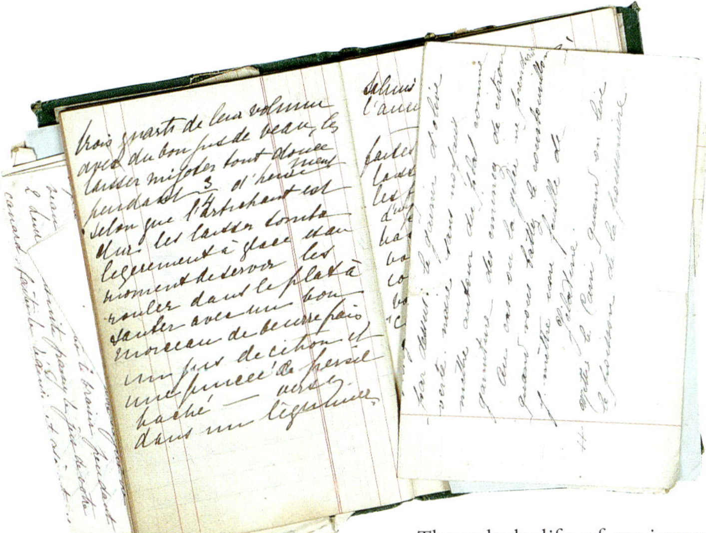

1732: 'Paid for some barrels for wine-making at Pommard, 4 1/2 'queux.' (The vineyard at Pommard owned by the Commarin estate is still there, and is called Commaraine).
1733: Paid for being the puppeteer for my son... paid for a basketful of bottles of Chalon (wine)... bought 300 bottles in order to send some wine to Germany.'

The whole life of an important family and its household is to be found within these important documents. There are no battles or disasters, but simply a life revolving around the château and countryside that not even the Revolution was able to tear apart. The 18th century apartments have not changed, neither has the library full of books that bear the Vienne-d'Antigny cipher. The great hall, which has seen so many family parties, is dominated by a portrait of Louis XV, whilst in Marie-Judith de Vienne's living room can still be seen an amusing painting that depicts Henry IV seducing, with the aid of his well-filled gamebag, Lady de Thoissy, a relative of the de Viennes. During the Revolution, Jacques de Damas, Marie-Judith's son, was arrested three times, but released three times. Commarin then passed on inheritance to the de Vogüé family, and is today the home of Count and Countess Louis de Vogüé, from whom we collected these original recipes. Some are well and truly local, whereas others come from further afield, just as it suited the old families. Once tried and adopted, they have become an integral part of the château's long and unbroken history.

BAKED POACHED EGGS AND MASHED POTATOES

Make some very runny mashed potato, and spread it out on a soup dish. Put your poached eggs on it, and cover with a second layer of mashed potatoes. Sprinkle with breadcrumbs, dot with some knobs of butter, and bake in the oven for 5 minutes.

EGG, HAM, AND CHEESE SOUFFLÉ TOASTS

To be served as a main course. Have ready some ham, some eggs (1 per person), some grated gruyère, some slightly stale bread, a frying pan, and some sunflower oil. Toast some slices of slightly stale bread, and, using a glass by way of a cutter, cut some round pieces out of it (1 per person), doing the same with the ham. Separate the egg yolks and whites. Put a little grated gruyère in with the egg yolks to thicken them, and season. Whisk the egg whites until very stiff. On each round of toast, put a slice of ham and a little of the egg yolks and gruyère, and top with a dome of whisked egg white. Heat the oil in a frying pan and put in the prepared rounds. Using a tablespoon, pour the oil gently and carefully over each dome. The oil must be very hot but not boiling or smoking.
The 'soufflé' swells and turns golden after being 'basted' several times.
Serve immediately.

CHICKEN AND 'FOIE GRAS' IN ASPIC

You need a good free-range chicken of about 2.5 kg, 1.5 litres meat jelly (either home-made or ordered from a 'charcuterie' or delicatessen), 200 g 'foie gras', a lot of vegetables, and a bouquet garni.
A 24 cm sandwich tin.
Start the cooking of the chicken in cold water with as many vegetables as possible – lots of carrots, a leek, 2 turnips, a stick of celery, thyme, bay leaves, lots of parsley, an onion studded with cloves, salt, and pepper. Cook for about 1.5 hours, after which, melt the jelly so that it is very hot but not boiling. This aspic must be worked with while hot, so that all the ingredients blend together and soak up all the flavours.
Remove the chicken skin, and finely slice the chicken into small, thin pieces.
Put a layer of jelly on the bottom of the sandwich tin, then a layer of chicken, putting some cubes of 'foie gras' into the gaps. Continue this process to make up to 4 layers, if possible, finishing with the jelly (remember to leave enough space for it).
Refrigerate for about 12 hours.
To remove from the tin, run a knife point between the edge of the aspic and the tin so that there is an intake of air.
Serve with a well-seasoned mixed salad.
This is dish is beyond compare, and is ideal, what is more, for parties and celebrations.
Don't hesitate to prepare it the night before or even longer beforehand because this very attractive dish freezes well.
This is the occasion to bring out a great white wine, a Corton-Charlemagne or Montrachet.

An 18th century cabbage made of Sceaux china.

Chicken and 'foie gras' in aspic.

CHESTER CAKES

1/4 lb flour
1/4 lb butter
60 g Parmesan cheese
60 g Cheshire cheese,
a bare pinch of salt,
and a hint of cayenne pepper.

Mix all the ingredients together. Leave the dough to rest for 2 hours., and then roll out two 1 cm-thick pieces of pastry. Bake in the oven, keeping an eye on the cooking.

Meanwhile, mix together 100 g butter, 100 g Cheshire cheese, and a dash of cayenne pepper. Combine to form a paste that you put between the two pieces of pastry, bake in a hot oven for a second, and serve.

DUCK PÂTÉ AND DUCK 'EN CROÛTE'

Remove all the bones from a good large duck, then marinade it all day in some madeira, cognac, thyme, bay leaves, a finely sliced onion, and a sliced carrot.

Then take some well-cleaned duck livers and some raw 'foie gras', put them on some scales, and, on the other side, put the same weight of pure pork fat.

Sauté the well-seasoned livers and pork fat in a frying pan for 7 or 8 minutes.

Then mince and sieve them.

Cover the duck with this mixture.

Make a very hard pâté pastry (see recipe below), and cover all your duck with the pastry. Cook for 2 hours in the oven.

Make some stock with the duck carcass and a piece of veal, adding the marinade for the duck.

When the pastry is cooked, slice off the top so as to make a lid in the pastry.

Lift it off and pour the stock over the pâté.

Place it on some ice or in a cool place.

This is better if made the day before it is to be eaten.

Pâté pastry:
1 litre flour,
15g salt,
1 egg,
1/4 lb butter,
1/2 glass of water.

Mix all this together.

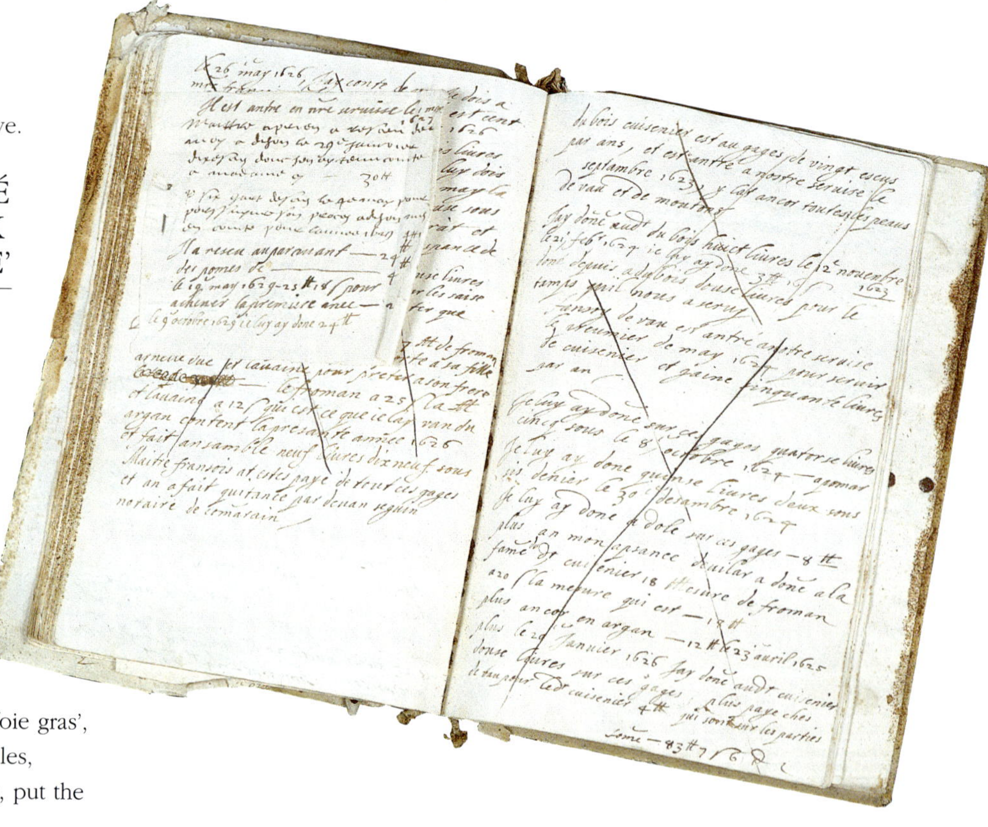

COURGETTE AND TOMATO GRATIN

Evenly slice some courgettes and tomatoes that have been washed but not peeled. Arrange in tightly-packed rows in a baking dish, alternating a slice of courgette and a slice of tomato on top of each other but leaving the top of each slice sticking out. Season, and add some chopped shallots, a lot of both curly and flat-leaved parsley, and a variety of aromatic herbs. Sprinkle well with olive oil. Put in the oven, keeping an eye on it while it cooks for a good 1/2 hour.

RIZ
CHICOREE
SUCRE

TANLAY

Where time stands still

The château of Tanlay's kitchen, full of the scents of autumn fruits.

Tanlay is one of those châteaux that is often described as a palace. This is not because of its size – there are, after all, larger châteaux – but because it has a certain grandeur that becomes increasingly evident right from the moment of arrival, from the surrounding wall, the bridge with its three arches, and the 16th century 'Portal' or 'little château', to the green courtyard enclosed by high walls with blind arcades. There are no protective barriers, simply a certain air of self-assurance. Two curious obelisks, decorated with bosses, act as symbolic sentry boxes, defending the bridge over the moat. The porter's lodge, which used to be joined to the two wings by a protective wall, gives access, at last, to the main courtyard. Are these symbolic defences meant to encourage us not to enter the château? What a good idea, because the park is truly splendid, planted with tall trees that dot the banks of the 526m-long royal canal. The countless views of the château will delight the lover of architecture... and bewilder the photographer! For our photograph, we have chosen the north side, which is less distinguished than the others, but just as ornate. When, from 1642 onwards, Marcel Particelli d'Hémery started rebuilding the old fortress that he had bought from Claude Vignier, who had acquired it through his wife, Catherine Chabot, heiress of the d'Andelot family, he chose the architect, Le Muet. Le Muet loved order and symmetry, but had to come to a compromise with the irregular shape of the old building with its encircling moat. This northern side, which seems to be the simplest, is note-worthy because of the alternating style of its dormer windows, some of which are 'bull's eye' in design, whereas others are triangular. As is well-known, the roof's timber framework was an innovation that enabled the construction of high gables to provide extra accommodation. Finally, the tall chimneys topped with pomegranates lighten the whole appearance of the building. This side also has a moat, and is closed by a 17th century iron gate brought from Quincy Abbey.

The northern side of the château of Tanlay.

The coat-of-arms of the Tanlay family, which stands on the corner of the front of the château. Jehan Thévenin, a councillor to the king, bought the Tanlay estate in 1704 from the descendants of the Particellis, and became the new Marquis of Tanlay. To these arms, we are going to quote the personal motto of Etienne de Tanlay (1750 - 1802), which can be interpreted in whichever way you like :
'In the world's ravine
Get to know the masculine.
In the world's valley,
Stick to the feminine.'

We go back into the château by the entrance hall of the Caesars, which is decorated with busts brought back from Italy in the 17th century. It leads on to another entrance hall, this one full of hunting souvenirs, as from 1780, Tanlay's household staff hunted wolves, wild boars, and stags. Among their accumulated hunting trophies are even some moose antlers that were brought back from Canada.
We were greeted by the Countess de La Chauvinière. The Count is the grandson of the last Marquis de Tanlay, a former ambassador and highly skilled and experienced fighter pilot, whose family bought the château in 1704.
Tanlay has always been well-maintained, and the passing centuries have been kind to it. Our recipes are those of the family, and have been set to music by Antoine d'Ormesson, a family friend.

The entrance hall displays the trophies of the hunting retinue of Etienne, marquis of Tanlay, which was established in 1780 and disbanded in 1931, and which hunted in the many forests of north-eastern Burgundy.

BREAD AND EGG SOUP

Break up some pieces of stale bread, put them into some cold water, add some salt, and boil over a low heat for about an hour. Add a knob of fresh butter and make some thickening for the soup with an egg. Cream or milk can also be added.

ECONOMICAL MACARONI LOAF

200 g macaroni,
1 litre milk,
125 g grated gruyère,
125 g cooked ham,
4 eggs, 50g butter.

Cook the macaroni in some boiling salted water. Add the butter, cheese, and diced cooked ham, as well as the beaten eggs.

Autumn in Burgundy is the season of the lovely aromatic scents of ripe quinces, mushrooms, and grapes. Tanlay's vineyard was quoted in the 19th century as producing 'tasty white wines that keep well.', but since then, phylloxera has ravaged and ruined this vineyard that lies close to Chablis. Today, however, vines are making a comeback all over the Tonnerre area. Chardonnay wines are very fruity and full-bodied, as well as making very good sparkling wines, although it is true to say that the Champagne region is only a stone's throw away.

The private dining room. Cats and dogs fight under the eye of the parrot, thanks to the brush of Jean-Baptiste Oudry. The sideboard is typical of the Burgundian Renaissance period. The beautiful crystal glasses are 17th century, and the dinner service bears the Tanlay arms.

Season, and cook in the oven in a greased tin. Remove the macaroni loaf from the tin, place on a plate, and pour a tomato sauce over it.

LETTUCE PURÉE

Take a good quantity of lettuce, wash it, and cook in boiling water, adding salt towards the end. Drain well, and pass through a sieve. Make a béchamel sauce and mix with the sieved lettuce.

BUTTER FOR SNAILS

For 100 snails:
1 lb butter, 8 g salt, 10 g finely chopped garlic, 15 g finely chopped parsley

HAM IN A CREAM SAUCE

Reduce the shallots in some vinegar. Add some stock, reduce it slightly, and add some tomato purée, a little curry, and some top-quality cream. Put the ham on a plate, pour the sauce over it, and cook in the oven.

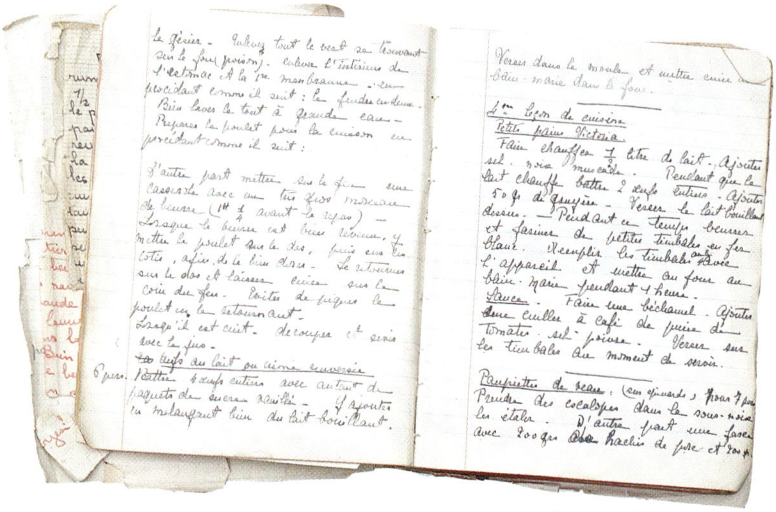

MARINADED VENISON 'OTHELLO'

'This is a recipe of one of the marquises of Tanlay who, as the palace's poet, imagined that one day a young fawn, feeling somewhat dazed, was following a path through Tanlay's park when it inadvertently found itself inside the château's oven, coming out as dark-skinned as Othello. It was in the Burgundian accent that rolls its 'r's, like the carriage wheels used to make on the stony paths in the vineyards, that one evening, being an honest man, he revealed the recipe so as to whet our appetites.'

A boned joint of venison, a venison bone, three thin slices of bacon, two truffles, a clove of garlic, parsley stalks, two thinly sliced shallots and three thinly sliced carrots, a spoonful of parsley, a spoonful of breadcrumbs, some rosemary, a bottle of Chablis, 1/2 litre of meat stock, a liqueur glassful of vinegar, two liqueur glassfuls of cognac, a spoonful of veal stock, oil and butter, salt and pepper.

Marinade the venison for 24 hours in 50 cl of Chablis, the liqueur glassful of vinegar, two tablespoonfuls of groundnut oil, thinly sliced shallots and carrots, parsley stalks, salt, and the venison bone chopped into pieces. At the end of the marinading time, drain the joint through a cloth and dry it well.

Rub it with garlic, and put the slices of bacon around it. Season.

Sieve the marinade, and heat gently to reduce it.

In a separate pan, brown the pieces of bone with part of the marinade vegetables, add them to the reduced marinade, and flambé all of it in a glassful of cognac. Sieve it all again. Add a spoonful of veal stock. Cook over a very low heat for about 15 minutes. Put half a glassful of marinade to one side, and keep the rest hot. Put the joint into a greased casserole dish with a cooking stock of a mixture of the other half-bottle of Chablis, 20 cl of stock, and half a glassful of marinade and cook in a medium oven, allowing

15 minutes per pound of meat. Add the rest of the stock gradually, basting the meat with it during the course of cooking.
Chop the parsley, and mix with the breadcrumbs and rosemary. Remove the joint from the casserole when cooked, and put on a greased baking plate, sprinkling it with the above mixture. Cook in the oven for a further 15 minutes, basting with the juices in the casserole. Pour the rest of the marinade into a casserole and add the residue of the cooking stock from the casserole. Reduce this, stirring constantly, and pour the sauce into a gravy-boat. Two spoonfuls of 'crème fraîche' may be added. Take the joint out of the oven, carve it into thin slices, and place them on a warmed plate. Pour the second glass of cognac onto them and flambé. Arrange slices of truffle that have been sautéed in butter around the meat.
A bottle of Romanée-Conti or, failing that, a good Vosne-Romanée, should complement this great dish in suitably aristocratic fashion.

Marinaded venison 'Othello'. The table pieces are made of Sèvres porcelain.

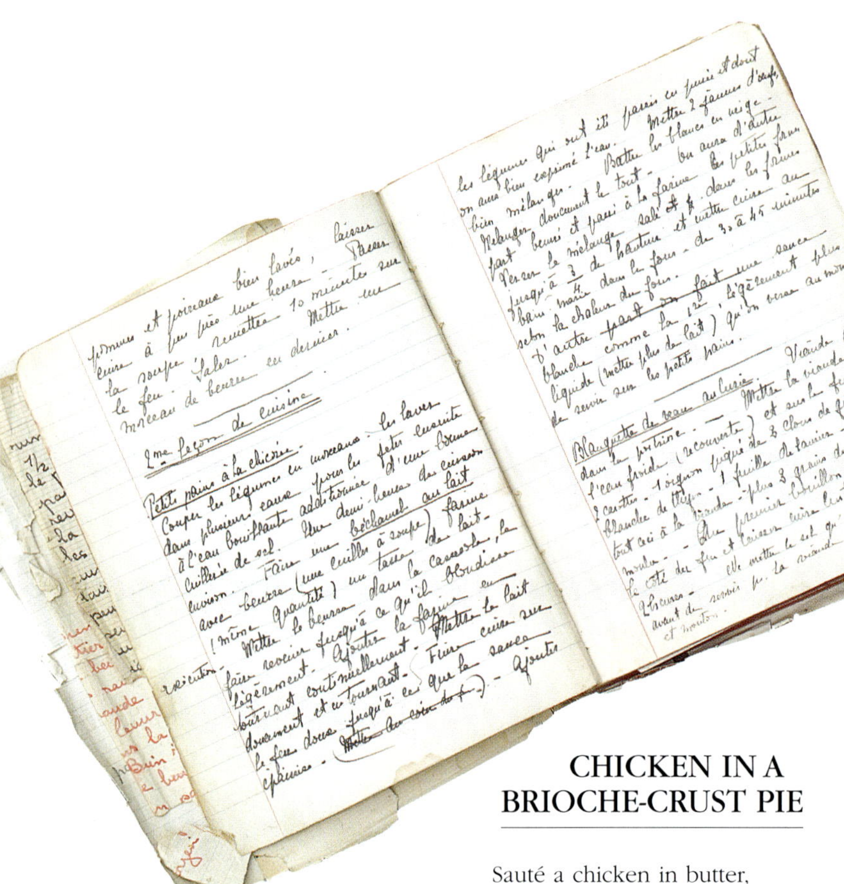

CHICKEN IN A BRIOCHE-CRUST PIE

Sauté a chicken in butter, season well, and then add 20 small onions and 20 mushroom tops. Cook together, and then, in an earthenware dish, place the chicken onto some potatoes cooked 'à l'anglaise' (boiled). Deglaze the pan with some madeira and double cream.
Pour all this over the chicken and cover the dish with a thin layer of brioche pastry.
Cook quickly and serve immediately.

ALMOND AND HAZELNUT BISCUITS

These keep for a very long time in an airtight tin.
Take 3 eggs,
150 g caster sugar,
150 g flour,
and the same weights of almonds and hazelnuts,
1 packet of vanilla sugar.
Shell and chop the almonds and hazelnuts.
Work together the eggs and sugar in a bowl with a palette knife.
Gradually add the sieved flour and the almond-hazelnut mixture.
Turn out the mixture onto a greased baking sheet.
It will spread out evenly by itself.
Bake for 35 minutes in a moderate oven.
As soon as it comes out of the oven, cut into diamond- or rectangular-shaped biscuits.

PIKE IN A CHABLIS SAUCE

Thoroughly grease a gratin dish in which you put three chopped shallots, some Chablis, and some strong fish stock. Add five chopped tomatoes, and your pike, slit open in the middle. Season. Allow 20 to 30 minutes cooking time in the oven, basting the pike frequently. Put the pike on a long dish. Beat some fresh butter in with the cooking juices. Sieve the sauce and pour it over the pike, decorating it with lemon slices and chopped parsley. Serve very hot.

The Tanlay hunting fanfare.

The Chablis can, of course, be replaced by a white Tonnerre, of which there are some very good wines, becoming fuller in flavour over two or three years.

APPLE AND POTATO GRATIN

This dish goes well with the venison recipe above.
In a greased gratin dish, make a layer of thinly sliced Reinette apples, and then a layer of thinly sliced potatoes that have been washed under running water to remove the starch. Season., and sprinkle with a light layer of grated Parmesan. Finish by repeating the two alternating layers. Season, and sprinkle with another layer of Parmesan. Cook in a medium oven for about 30 minutes.

CHOCOLATE CAKE WITH A BUTTER CREAM FILLING

This cake is easy enough to be made by a beginner.
You need a 22 cm cake tin that is 6 cm deep:
4 eggs, 100 g sugar,
140 g chocolate,
30 g cream of tartar.
Grease and flour the tin. Stir four egg yolks and the sugar together in a bowl until the mixture forms a long ribbon when dropped from the spoon, and then add 140 g of softened chocolate. Stir again and add the whisked egg whites, flour, and cream of tartar. Pour the mixture into the tin, and bake in a low oven for about 30 minutes.
Leave the cake to cool thoroughly, and meanwhile make the following filling:
Beat the butter in a bowl until soft and smooth, then beat in 30 g icing sugar followed by 70 g chocolate powder. Mix well to a smooth and creamy consistency. Slice the cake in half horizontally, spread the cream evenly over the lower half with a palette knife, and gently replace the top half of the cake.

Epoisses

A tranquil château

A horseshoe-shaped château, which is the result of centuries of construction, but also of destruction - such is the present-day appearance of Epoisses.

History has transformed the fortress of Epoisses into a peaceful château, whose semi-circular structure lies within the old fortifications. The moat has been filled in, the towers demolished, and the park is now a playground for the village schoolchildren. However, this is only the final chapter of a troubled and extremely eventful history.

First of all, in the 6th century, there was the formidable Queen Brunehault, who was regent for her grandson, Thierry, the king of Burgundy. The queen had ambitions of her own and did not want to hand over the throne to Thierry, so she kept him away by providing him with a court of women of easy virtue and lots of good food and drink. The great St Colomba, who had come over from Ireland to the monastery at Luxeuil, journeyed to Epoisses to reprimand the king for his bad behaviour. Brunehault and Thierry tried to win him over by preparing a magnificent banquet for him, but St Colomba cursed them so much that the dishes on the table shattered.

A very long time later, Epoisses, which belonged to the dukes of Burgundy, passed into the ownership of the Count of Montbard, then, through inheritance, to the Mello family, in whose possession it remained from 1237 to 1421, when ownership passed to the Montagus. After

The beautiful Cleopatra once bet her lover, Antony, one of Rome's governing triumvirate, that she could eat a fortune's worth of a meal. She can be seen on this tapestry, winning her bet... by dissolving the finest of pearls in vinegar. Surrounded by wood panelling in the style of Louis XIV, another of the Sun's children, she watches over the château of Epoisses' meals, which may be more modest, but are very much more appetising!

the death of Claude de Montagu, Duke Charles the Bold had his chancellor, Hugonet, purchase Epoisses. This, however, was at the time when King Louis XI of France was busy scheming to bring the duchy under French control, and he had Hugonet murdered and his estate seized. Epoisses passed to the Duchess Mary, and then again to Louis XI, who gave it to the Marshal of Hochberg. Among successive owners were some distinguished personalities, such as Louis of Orleans, Duke of Longueville and companion of Louis XII; Jacques of Savoy, Duke of Nemours and companion of Henry II, who sold Epoisses in 1561 to the Marshal de Bourdillon; and Louis d'Anssienville, who was forced to abandon Epoisses during the French Wars of Religion, and who later bought back the fortifications that had been erected against him. He was made Marquis of Epoisses in 1613 by King Louis XIII. Finally, there was Guillaume de Pechpeyrou, Count of Comminges and Guitaut, Marquis of Epoisses, and Louis d'Anssienville's grandson. Over three centuries later, this family, which originally came from Quercy, still live in the château of Epoisses.

This history unfolds against a background of wars between France and Burgundy, of sackings and Crusades, of visits by distinguished personalities, even of the Great Condé, who was lord of Epoisses between 1669 and 1672 on behalf of Guillaume de Guitaut. The Marquise de Sévigné often stayed here, paying neighbourly visits from her estate at Bourbilly, and entertaining her hosts with the wit made famous in her letters, after having drunk too much good Burgundy.

The present-day appearance of the château is, however, a consequence of the French Revolution. At the time of the Revolution, it was an 8-sided fortress, of which the first surrounding wall had already been levelled. The Committee for Public Safety ordered Charles de Guitaut to demolish half the building, allowing him to keep the other half, and it is this that we see today, the rubble from the demolished half being used to fill in the moat. This 'half château' has, nonetheless, a proud and noble appearance, bearing traces of the different stages of its construction. There is the curious balcony that was constructed in a single day so that the Prince de Condé could see his woods from his house when he returned from hunting. The fore-court has kept its houses and outbuildings, the dovecote with its three thousand holes, the parish church, and the Epoisses village school.

The château's interior depicts its history, with its entrance hall decorated with the coats-of-arms of successive owners, the picture gallery hung with portraits of famous men, the king's bedroom, where, of course, Henry IV would have slept, as well as the bedroom of Madame de Sévigné, who wrote, 'This house is surprisingly large and beautiful'. During the demolition work, the prison, the pilgrims' hall, and the knights' hall all disappeared. What remains is the pleasant, sunny part, guarded today by some very good-natured dogs.

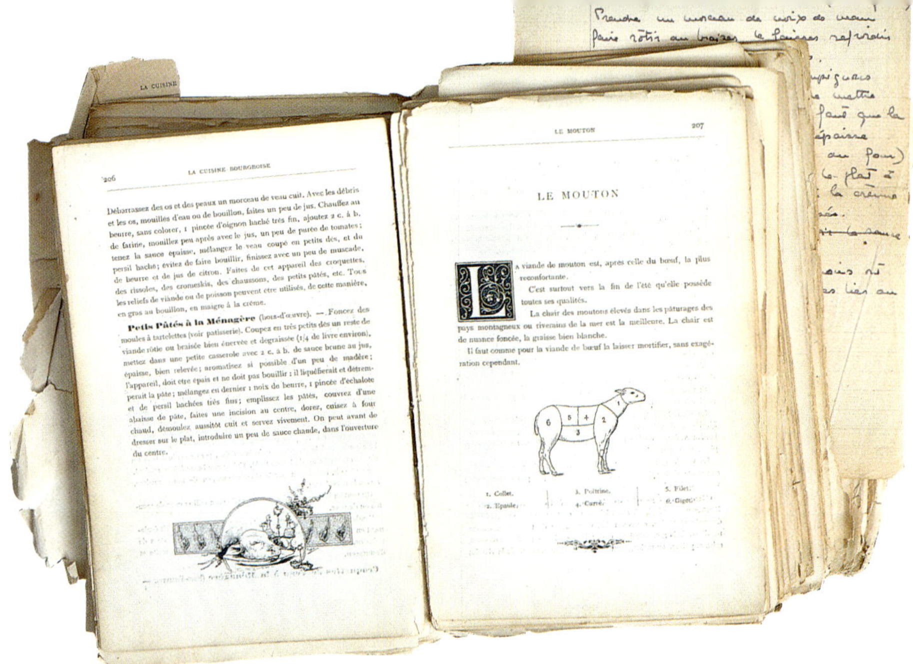

Jean de Gouy was the chef for Madame d'Ursel, Marguerite de Guitaut's grandmother. Here are some recipes from the book that he published in 1895.

MULLED BEER

This hot mulled beer is also often served at the Austro-Hungarian court during rest-breaks in the hunting.
Bring to the boil 4 litres of bock beer or Pilsen, 1/2 litre of sugar, a cinnamon stick, a piece of lemon peel, chopped ginger root.
Put 12 egg yolks in a bowl, and mix them with 2 dl of rum or Slibovitz (grain gin).
Add the beer, heat well, but without letting it boil, whisking vigorously.
At the last minute, pour in 2 demi-litres of madeira and 1/2 lb high-quality butter, cut into small pieces.
As soon as this has melted, pour the drink through a fine sieve. Serve in small cups.

BOILED POTATOES

A basic recipe, yet even so, the potato (pomme de terre) deserves to be treated well, especially when it has such a pretty name!

The potatoes must be well-covered with water, and brought to a boil that is constant without being too fierce. Drain carefully as soon as they are cooked. Put them, uncovered, over the heat and toss them to dry.
If you are not going to serve them immediately, do not

cover them completely.
'Old' potatoes must not be cooked in the same way as new potatoes.
New potatoes often contain more water, and must not be peeled until the last minute, and then cooked in boiling water in order to close the pores.
'Old' potatoes that are wrinkled and sprouting have a sour taste, and must be peeled several hours in advance and heated up in cold water.

FRIED SMALL FRESHWATER FISH

Not all small fish need gutting. Clean them, dip them in some milk, and then some flour. Shake well. Immerse them in a bath of boiling oil for a few minutes. Drain, and serve immediately.

FISH IN ANCHOVY SAUCE

Carefully remove the skin and bones from 1/2 kg of fish, thinly slice it, and add 1/4 kg of breadcrumbs and 2 eggs. Season with 2 spoonfuls of English-style anchovy sauce (a roux of 60 g butter and 60 g flour, 3/4 litre of boiling salted water, a few drops of lemon juice, 200 g of butter, and some anchovy essence). Put into a plain greased mould, and cook for 1/2 hour in a bain-marie. Serve with an anchovy butter sauce.

SNAILS IN A WHITE WINE SAUCE

If the snails have been fed during the last month, put them in a tub with a good handful of coarse salt and 2 or 3 demi-litres of ordinary vinegar.
Half an hour later, wash them thoroughly several times, until there is no longer any scum. Throw them into some boiling salted water to which has been added some wood ash and some bicarbonate of soda.

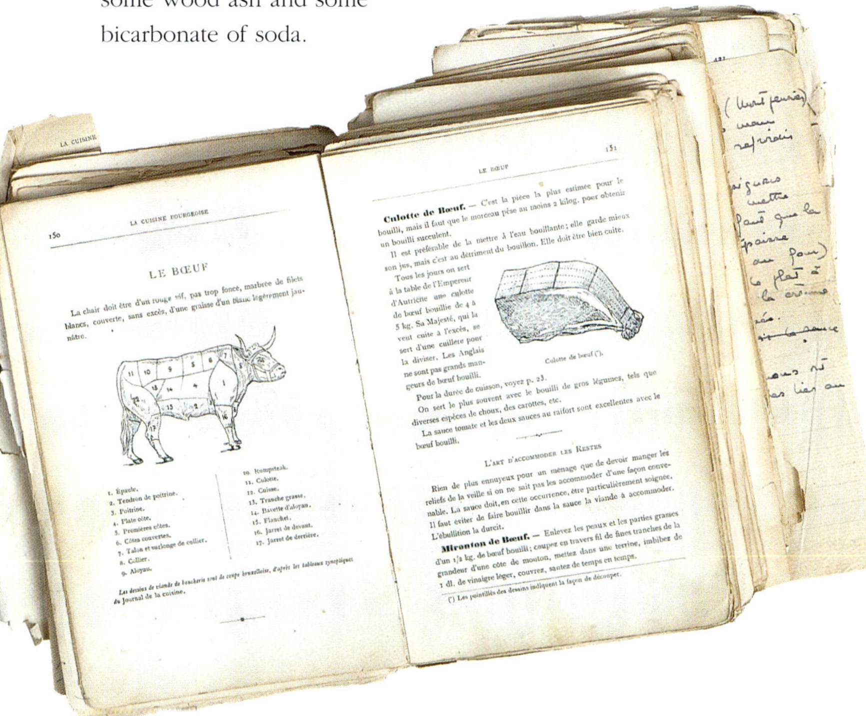

150 LA CUISINE BOURGEOISE

LE BŒUF

La chair doit être d'un rouge vif, pas trop foncé, marbrée de filets blancs, couverte, sans excès, d'une graisse d'un blanc légèrement jaunâtre.

1. Épaule.
2. Tendron de poitrine.
3. Poitrine.
4. Plate côte.
5. Premières côtes.
6. Côtes couvertes.
7. Talon et surlonge de collier.
8. Collier.
9. Aloyau.
10. Rumpsteak.
11. Culotte.
12. Cuisse.
13. Tranche grasse.
14. Bavette d'aloyau.
15. Flanchet.
16. Jarret de devant.
17. Jarret de derrière.

Les dessins de viande de boucherie sont de coupe bruxelloise, d'après les tableaux synoptiques du Journal de la cuisine.

LE BŒUF 151

Culotte de Bœuf. — C'est la pièce la plus estimée pour le bouilli, mais il faut que le morceau pèse au moins 2 kilog. pour obtenir un bouilli succulent.

Il est préférable de la mettre à l'eau bouillante; elle garde mieux son jus, mais c'est au détriment du bouillon. Elle doit être bien cuite.

Tous les jours on sert à la table de l'Empereur d'Autriche une culotte de bœuf bouillie de 4 à 5 kg. Sa Majesté, qui la veut cuite à l'excès, se sert d'une cuillère pour la diviser. Les Anglais ne sont pas grands mangeurs de bœuf bouilli.

Culotte de bœuf (*).

Pour la durée de cuisson, voyez p. 23.

On sert le plus souvent avec le bouilli de gros légumes, tels que diverses espèces de choux, des carottes, etc.

La sauce tomate et les deux sauces au raifort sont excellentes avec le bœuf bouilli.

L'Art d'accommoder les Restes

Rien de plus ennuyeux pour un ménage que de devoir manger les reliefs de la veille si on ne sait pas les accommoder d'une façon convenable. La sauce doit, en cette occurrence, être particulièrement soignée. Il faut éviter de faire bouillir dans la sauce la viande à accommoder. L'ébullition la durcit.

Mironton de Bœuf. — Enlevez les peaux et les parties grasses d'un 1/2 kg. de bœuf bouilli; coupez en travers fil de fines tranches de la grandeur d'une côte de mouton, mettez dans une terrine, imbibez de 1 dl. de vinaigre léger, couvrez, sautez de temps en temps.

(*) Les pointillés des dessins indiquent la façon de découper.

Jean de Gouy's recipe book.

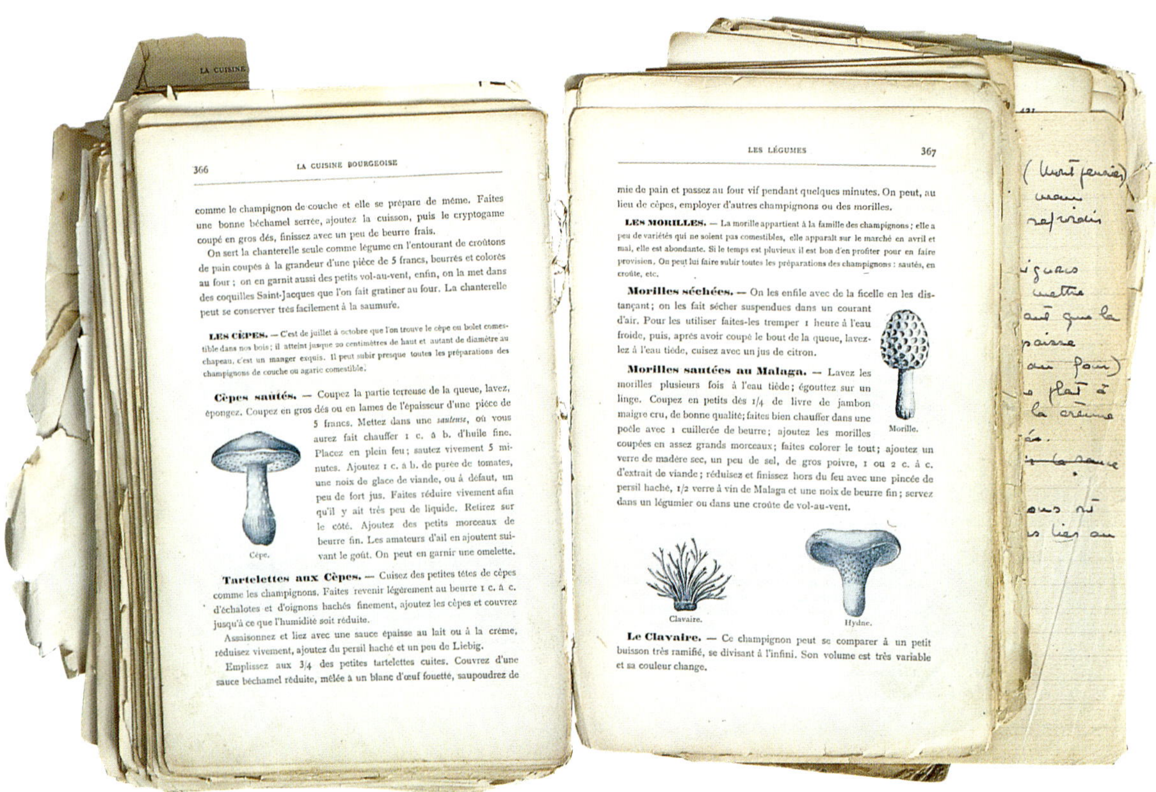

366 LA CUISINE BOURGEOISE

comme le champignon de couche et elle se prépare de même. Faites une bonne béchamel serrée, ajoutez la cuisson, puis le cryptogame coupé en gros dés, finissez avec un peu de beurre frais.

On sert la chanterelle seule comme légume en l'entourant de croûtons de pain coupés à la grandeur d'une pièce de 5 francs, beurrés et colorés au four ; on en garnit aussi des petits vol-au-vent, enfin, on la met dans des coquilles Saint-Jacques que l'on fait gratiner au four. La chanterelle peut se conserver très facilement à la saumure.

LES CÈPES. — C'est de juillet à octobre que l'on trouve le cèpe ou bolet comestible dans nos bois ; il atteint jusque 20 centimètres de haut et autant de diamètre au chapeau, c'est un manger exquis. Il peut subir presque toutes les préparations des champignons de couche ou agaric comestible.

Cèpes sautés. — Coupez la partie terreuse de la queue, lavez, épongez. Coupez en gros dés ou en lames de l'épaisseur d'une pièce de 5 francs. Mettez dans une *sauteuse*, où vous aurez fait chauffer 1 c. à b. d'huile fine. Placez en plein feu ; sautez vivement 5 minutes. Ajoutez 1 c. à b. de purée de tomates, une noix de glace de viande, ou à défaut, un peu de fort jus. Faites réduire vivement afin qu'il y ait très peu de liquide. Retirez sur le côté. Ajoutez des petits morceaux de beurre fin. Les amateurs d'ail en ajoutent suivant le goût. On peut en garnir une omelette.

Cèpe.

Tartelettes aux Cèpes. — Cuisez des petites têtes de cèpes comme les champignons. Faites revenir légèrement au beurre 1 c. à c. d'échalotes et d'oignons hachés finement, ajoutez les cèpes et couvrez jusqu'à ce que l'humidité soit réduite.

Assaisonnez et liez avec une sauce épaisse au lait ou à la crème, réduisez vivement, ajoutez du persil haché et un peu de Liebig.

Emplissez aux 3/4 des petites tartelettes cuites. Couvrez d'une sauce béchamel réduite, mêlée à un blanc d'œuf fouetté, saupoudrez de

LES LÉGUMES 367

mie de pain et passez au four vif pendant quelques minutes. On peut, au lieu de cèpes, employer d'autres champignons ou des morilles.

LES MORILLES. — La morille appartient à la famille des champignons ; elle a peu de variétés qui ne soient pas comestibles, elle apparaît sur le marché en avril et mai, elle est abondante. Si le temps est pluvieux il est bon d'en profiter pour en faire provision. On peut lui faire subir toutes les préparations des champignons : sautés, en croûte, etc.

Morilles séchées. — On les enfile avec de la ficelle en les distançant ; on les fait sécher suspendues dans un courant d'air. Pour les utiliser faites-les tremper 1 heure à l'eau froide, puis, après avoir coupé le bout de la queue, lavez-lez à l'eau tiède, cuisez avec un jus de citron.

Morilles sautées au Malaga. — Lavez les morilles plusieurs fois à l'eau tiède ; égouttez sur un linge. Coupez en petits dés 1/4 de livre de jambon maigre cru, de bonne qualité ; faites bien chauffer dans une poêle avec 1 cuillerée de beurre ; ajoutez les morilles coupées en assez grands morceaux ; faites colorer le tout ; ajoutez un verre de madère sec, un peu de sel, de gros poivre, 1 ou 2 c. à c. d'extrait de viande ; réduisez et finissez hors du feu avec une pincée de persil haché, 1/2 verre à vin de Malaga et une noix de beurre fin ; servez dans un légumier ou dans une croûte de vol-au-vent.

Morille.

Clavaire.

Hydne.

Le Clavaire. — Ce champignon peut se comparer à un petit buisson très ramifié, se divisant à l'infini. Son volume est très variable et sa couleur change.

Drain after 10 minutes,
and take the snails
out of their shells.
Cook them in a mixture
of half water and half white
wine, or in some stock,
and add flavour
to the recipe
with a bouquet garni
and some peppercorns.
Put the snails back
into their well-cleaned
shells and fill
the shells with
a beurre manié mixed
with parsley,
chopped shallots,
and a touch of garlic.
Cook for 5 minutes
in a hot oven.

BROAD BEANS

The smallest beans are the best.
If they are big, they must be
shelled before cooking.
They are cooked in boiling
water, drained, covered
with a runny milk sauce,
and, as a final touch, topped
at the last minute with a little
fresh butter and some
chopped savory.

KIDNEY BEAN SOUP

Soak some red kidney beans
in some rainwater overnight.
Drain.
Put them in cold water
and bring to the boil, adding
salt only halfway through
the cooking time, because,
as is the case for all dried
vegetables, the addition
of salt at the beginning
makes them tough.
Add a little 'mirepoix'
(diced ham, carrots,
onions, thyme,
and bay leaves,
which have been browned
a little in butter).
Cook slowly.
Strain the sauce, and make
it thinner, if necessary,
so as to get a clear purée.
Add a glass of red Burgundy
to it before serving.

The private kitchen. This is a cheerful place where each member of the family has his own place and his own table napkin, some of which belonged to the family's ancestors, and, as is the case with jewels, are handed down to the grandchildren.

SUMMER SNOW

In a bowl,
whisk 6 egg whites
until very stiff.
Very gently
add 1/4 litre of sweetened
whipped cream,
4 drops of lemon essence,
1 demi-litre of pale sherry,
and 2 teaspoonfuls
of rose-water.
Stand the bowl
in ice immediately,
and then pour into
some well-chilled
champagne glasses.

Epoisses cheese quiche.

Today's recipes at the château of Epoisses

EPOISSES CHEESE QUICHE

What could be more natural at Epoisses?
This internationally renowned cheese is made exclusively in this small village. It is a soft cheese made from the Auxois region's high-quality cow's milk, and is cured by rubbing the rind in Marc de Bourgogne (a spirit distilled from grape residue after grape-pressing). It is a strong-flavoured cheese, and was a great favourite with Napoleon, who used to eat it with a glass of watered down Chambertin. Moreover, strong red cheeses go well with Epoisses, for instance, Beauclair, which is only an ungraded Epoisses, and which is just as delicious.

You need some ordinary shortcrust pastry, with which you line a flan tin.

Beat 6 eggs with a 20 cl pot of 'crème fraîche', add a mixture of cheeses comprising 1/3 Emmenthal and 2/3 crumbled Epoisses. Season to taste, and bake for about 30 minutes.

DUCK WITH TURNIPS

Pluck and clean a duck, and brown it well in sunflower oil. Add a little water or (even better) stock, and cook over a low heat.

Add a bouquet garni, and then the peeled turnips that have been cut up into pieces. Simmer for about 1,5 hours. Carve the duck and serve it with the slightly caramelised turnips arranged around it. Why not serve a Santenay with the 'canard aux navets' ?

ORANGE CAKE

4 eggs,
250 g sugar,
230 g flour,
160 g butter,
1 packet baking powder,
and 4 oranges.

Mix the egg yolks with the sugar and the juice of 3 oranges. Add the melted butter, baking powder, and flour. Whisk the egg whites until they form stiff peaks, and blend into the mixture. Pour into a greased cake tin and bake for 30 minutes in a medium oven. Take the cake out of the tin when cooked. Mix a little icing sugar with the juice of the 4th orange, and spread it over the cake while it is still warm. Leave to cool.

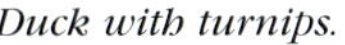

Duck with turnips.

Sully

The most beautiful courtyard in France

The fruits of the vegetable garden in Sully's kitchen: pumpkins, gourds, red and green cabbages, custard marrows, Sully-grown oranges, quinces, apples, nuts, and aromatic herbs from the garden: rosemary, chives, sage, savory, flat and curly parsley, dill, and lavender.

Jean-Baptiste de Mac-Mahon, a young doctor who had taken refuge in France, arrived, quite by chance, in Autun, following the completion of his studies in Paris. Although descended from the kings of Ireland, he was poor, but he managed to set himself up as a doctor in Autun. His growing reputation led to his treating Jean-Baptiste de Morey, whose wealthy family had bought Sully in 1714. Although Morey was an old man, he remarried, his second wife being his cousin, Charlotte Le Belin, who was 40 years younger than him. After her husband's death, Charlotte married the young doctor.

The couple had seven children, of whom Charles-Laure, Marquis de Mac-Mahon, entertained guests and hunted at Sully, but died unmarried, whilst Maurice-François had nine children. Jean-Baptiste de Mac-Mahon died before the Revolution, and it was his widow who strove, both during and after her lifetime to prevent the confiscation of the château. She first of all hired two volunteer guards, and then, when, in spite of everything, she was arrested, she was able to avoid being moved to Paris because of her great age and to return to Sully, where she died peacefully in 1798, at the age of 89. As a consequence of her death, the château should have been seized, but her death was concealed. Whenever a search was announced, the marquise was put into her bed, being hidden away again afterwards in a trough full of 'eau-de-vie' ('water of life' - brandy), which here certainly deserved its name! Thus, as a result of this hoax, the old marquise managed to hold on to Sully.

This Gien pottery plate commemorates the taking of Malakoff by Mac-Mahon. The Crimean War was a 19th century crusade, in which the French, English, and Piedmontese, reinforced by Turkish troops (Turkey at the time being called 'the sick man of Europe'), fought the Russian army of Tsar Nicholas I. When General Mac-Mahon had captured the fort of Malakoff, he uttered the famous cry of 'I'm here, and I'm staying here.', and so he did. After a year-long siege, The fall of Sebastopol gave victory to the Allies. In 1859, following the battle of Magenta against the Sardinian army, Mac-Mahon was awarded his marshal's baton and the title of Duke of Magenta.

Her two sons, who had left France at the time of the Revolution, later returned to the château. Maurice-François had a son, Charles-Marie, who was a keen hunter, and who died as a result of a fall from a horse in 1845. His son, Charles, succeeded him, followed by his son, Charles-Marie, who married Marthe de Vogüé, and who restored the south side of the château. The senior branch of the family died out with her in 1923.

Maurice, François-Maurice's other son, who was born in 1808, was never the château's owner. He was a graduate of the Saint-Cyr military academy, and had a brilliant military career that took him to the front line all over

Europe and Algeria. He was made a duke and a marshal, was wounded at Sedan during the Franco-Prussian war, was an opponent of the Paris Commune, and became president of the Republic in 1872. He resigned from this post in 1879, and died in 1893. His grandson, Maurice, inherited Sully on the death of his cousin, the Duchess Marthe. The château is owned today by his son, Philippe, Marquis of Mac-Mahon and Duke of Magenta.

However, Sully's history started well before that. There are still traces of Gauthier de Sully's 13th century fortified manor house, after which the estate passed to the Montagus, whose last heiress married Hugues de Rabutin. This family is very well-known in Burgundy, in particular because of Roger de Bussy-Rabutin (1618 – 1693), whose impertinence at court earned him a long period of exile in the château that bears his name. He was the author of 'Histoire Amoureuse des Gaules' (An Amorous History of the Gauls), and he embellished his château with portraits and mottoes that are scathing in their sarcasm.

The massive entrance door really does show that it belongs to a family of hunters, and even the door-bell is in the form of a stag's hoof.

In 1515, Christophe de Rabutin sold the Sully estate to Jean de Saulx and Marguerite de Tavannes, whose son, Guillaume, was as passionate in his love of hunting as he was in the fight against the Calvinists. His second son, Gaspard, a Marshal of France, pursued the Huguenots even more relentlessly, and initiated the château's reconstruction, work that was continued by his widow. Gaspard left two sons, Guillaume and Jehan, who fought on opposite sides throughout the Wars of Religion. Jehan, who was dismissed from his position as marshal by Henry IV, ended his days at Sully, whose reconstruction had been completed, and where he had inscribed in the great gallery, 'It is an honour to possess neither command nor estate in this reign!'

The two branches of the Saulx-Tavannes family fought a legal battle over the château until 1714, when Charles-Henry de Saulx sold Sully to the four Morey brothers. The Mac-Mahon family was soon going to make its entrance into Sully's history.

The most beautiful courtyard in France

The interior courtyard.

From the gate crowned by the Mac-Mahon cipher and from the far end of a long forecourt, the grand and impressive château comes into view. The balustrade of the stone bridge is decorated with cannon-balls and stone pyramids, which look like the jewelled setting, sprinkled there by giants, of a marquis' gigantic coronet. The door is bright blue and, like the stag's hoof that acts as a door-bell, is a reminder of the family's love of hunting. The massive, square-shaped château is encircled by a wide moat, which 200 years ago was empty and used for the keeping of boars, deer, and other wild animals.

Each side of the château has its own story to tell. The west side has remained unaltered since the 17th century. A bridge leads to a grand doorway on top of which is a floor with mullion windows framed with rectangular columns, and then by a wide pediment. The east side, which was altered during the 19th century, used to be linked to the other side of the moat by a bridge, and looks out over the Autunois countryside. The south side, where the raised form of the chapel exterior can be seen, was altered in about 1830 in the Neo-Gothic style, and then again in the late 19th century in a less overelaborate style.

The distinctive feature of Sully is to have its four corner towers positioned at an angle to the adjoining walls. However, the north side, which was built in the 18th century, takes in the corners of these towers, and it is this which gives it the real feel of a palace. Laid out in the classical style, it opens out onto a large terrace which juts out into the moat in a semi-circle. A final staircase plunges into the water.

Parties and grand balls spring to mind when you see this part of the château!
Hidden behind the exterior of this great vessel at anchor is an interior courtyard that Bussy-Rabutin, the 17th century general and poet, said was the most beautiful in France. This layout is common in fortified châteaux, but in a number of large châteaux a wing has been demolished in order to open out the view over the park. Sully has preserved its mystery, and its courtyard of a hundred windows. The Renaissance decoration with its bosses on the ground level, and its large arched openings and windows framed by Ionic columns on the floor above, transport us into another century. Orange trees ripen here. You find yourself awaiting the return of Gauthier, who was held prisoner on the island of Rhodes, of Guillaume and Jehan de Saulx, arm in arm, of Jean-Baptiste de Mac-Mahon coming to treat Morey, of the old marquise freed from Saulieu, or of Charles-Marie, the passionately keen hunter, in the company of his friend, the Marquis de Foudras. 'I had heard stories told which at the time I found hard to believe about the way that the Marquis de Mac-Mahon hunted, concerning wild boars hunted to the point of exhaustion, deer chased until they dropped from suffocation in forty minutes, hounds like hares…'

A view of the west side of the château, by with the main entrance door, and of the south side, which was remodelled twice during the 19th century.

Recipes from the château of SULLY

PUMPKIN SOUP

For about a kilo of pumpkin, you need two onions, salt and pepper, a tablespoonful of tomato purée, and some fresh nutmeg.
Cube the pumpkin, and finely slice the onions. Put it all into a saucepan, add enough water to cover, and season. Stir in the tomato purée and cook gently for 45 minutes. Then liquidise the soup, and add nutmeg to taste.

CHEESE CHOUX PUFFS

For 18 gougères:
25 cl water,
1/2 teaspoonful salt,
75 g butter, cut into pieces,
150 g flour, 4 medium eggs,
200 g grated Gruyère.

Boil the water in a saucepan with the salt and butter. As soon as the butter has melted, pour in all the flour at once and beat over a low heat until the mixture comes away from the sides of the pan. Remove from the heat and beat in a whole egg. Return the pan to the heat so as to dry the mixture, and then repeat the procedure for the three remaining eggs. Add the grated Gruyère. Grease a baking sheet, and, using a spoon, shape the dough into mounds of choux pastry. Cook for 25 minutes in a medium oven (thermostat 5/6). Do not open the oven door during the cooking time.

Gougères and Chassagne-Montrachet Abbaye de Morgeot, a 'premier cru' wine from the Marquis de Mac-Mahon's estate.

PHEASANT WITH CABBAGE

For 4 people:
A pheasant, a white cabbage, two onions, salt, pepper, and some bay leaves.
Brown the pheasant all over in a cast-iron casserole, together with the onions. Season. Cover and cook gently for about 1 1/2 hours. Meanwhile, thinly slice the cabbage, put in a pan, season, add some bay leaves, and steam gently for 15 minutes. Add the cabbage to the pheasant and simmer for another 5 minutes.

Pheasant with cabbage.

RED CABBAGE WITH APPLES

For 4 people:
a red cabbage, salt, pepper, three apples, and a tablespoonful of redcurrant jelly.
Thinly slice the cabbage. Peel and quarter the apples. Steam gently for 15 minutes, season, and then add the redcurrant jelly.

This colourful vegetable dish is served here in the serving dish that Mac-Mahon took to the Elysée when he became President of the Republic in 1872. It bears the initials M.M., a marquis' coronet, and a marshal's batons.

Red cabbage with apples.

QUINCE JELLY

Wipe the quinces clean, and quarter them.
Put them into a casserole and cook gently for 1 hour.
Strain off the juice.
Weigh the juice and add the same quantity of sugar.
Cook for 25 minutes.
Check to see whether it is cooked by pouring a little jelly onto a plate.
It should set immediately.
Remove from the heat and bottle.

QUINCE JELLIES

Take the reserved quince pulp, and for each kilo of pulp weigh out a kilo of sugar. Put into a preserving pan, and gently cook to remove moisture from the mixture. The mixture is ready when it comes away from the sides of the pan.
Spread it out onto a dish and leave it to dry for 8 days. Cut it into squares and coat with sugar.

SCOTTISH SCONES

250 g self-raising flour, baking powder, 50 g butter. Depending on the recipe required, sugar, spices, raisins, grated cheese, mustard, or treacle can be added.
To make a dozen small scones, take:

This handsome stone fireplace has changed along with the improvements made in the large kitchen in the basement. Used for extracting the fumes from the cast-iron stove, it also has a bread oven and a plate-warmer. Behind it, a complicated system of flaps regulates the rate of fuel combustion in the stove. Such a large house of course has cellars, storerooms, cold rooms, and a staff dining room.

The practical does not have to exclude the beautiful, charming caryatids decorating the corners of this handsome stove.

about 250 g of flour, add a small spoonful of baking powder, and sieve together.
For spiced scones, add a little sugar, some cinnamon and ginger, and 50 g of butter, cut into small pieces.
Rub the butter into the flour, using your fingertips, until the mixture looks crumbly.
For cheese scones, add some grated cheese, and for the other varieties, add some raisins.
Add enough milk to make a soft, slightly sticky dough. (Mix the milk with a spoonful of mustard for cheese scones, and with a spoonful of treacle for treacle scones. The exact quantity depends on your personal taste.)
Turn out the dough on a floured table and roll it out. (the less the dough is handled, the better the scones will be).

Cut out some small rounds of dough a few centimetres thick, and place them on a greased baking sheet (or on greaseproof paper). To make the scones more attractive, brush them with some milk or beaten egg. Bake the scones in a hot oven (mark 7) for about 10 minutes. Remove them from the oven before they are too cooked, and serve straightaway. Cut them in two, and eat spread with butter, thick fresh farmhouse cream, or home-made jam.

The painting in the dining room depicts the marquis, Charles-Marie, in the company of the Marquis de Foudras, and of his celebrated master of hounds, Racot.

The history of cooking intermingles with that of nations, and so, a number of dishes bear the names of important people who have played a military or political role in their country's history. 'Oeufs Magenta', 'Magentas', and 'Charlotte Malakoff' are three such dishes.

EGGS WITH A SALMON AND TRUFFLE FILLING

Shell some hard-boiled eggs, and trim off the ends so that they stand upright. Remove the yolks through this opening. Mix a little minced salmon with some thick mayonnaise to which chopped truffles have been added. Fill the eggs with this mixture, and arrange them on a plate. Fill the middle of the plate with the mayonnaise and truffles, pour a little liquid aspic over it, and leave it to set in a cool place. Decorate with prawns and slices of truffles.

These delicate Murano glasses bear the Mac-Mahon arms.

PRALINE SWEETS

These little sweets can no longer be found. They were made with crushed praline (a mixture of chopped almonds in brown caramel), which were then divided into small olive-shaped pieces. They were dipped in a very hot coffee fondant and then rolled immediately in crystallised sugar.

ALMOND CREAM CHARLOTTE

The siege of Malakoff took place during the Crimean War, and it was here that General Malakoff uttered the famous phrase, 'I'm here, and I'm staying here.'

125 g almonds,
125 g caster sugar,
125 g good quality butter,
125 g whipped cream,
vanilla, and kirsch.

Take about fifteen sponge fingers, trim off one of the ends so that they stand upright around a charlotte mould, ensuring that they are tightly packed together. Over the bottom of the mould should be a round piece of white paper. Having thus prepared the mould,

Away from the large reception rooms, Sully has smaller, cosier rooms, such as in this watchtower, where tea for a few guests can be served. On the table are quince jellies and the Duchess Amélie de Magenta's Scottish scones.

crush the almonds very finely, adding gradually a little sugar and powdered vanilla. When the almonds are well crushed, mix them with the slightly softened butter and work the whole mixture with a mortar and pestle to whiten and cream it. Add a liqueur glassful of good kirsch, and then put it into a bowl and blend in the whipped cream.

Pour this cream into the biscuit-lined mould, and leave in a cool place for several hours. When the charlotte has set, trim off the ends of the biscuits that jut out over it,

and turn it out onto a dish. Remove the circle of paper, and, using a fluted nozzle, pipe vanilla-flavoured whipped cream over the top.

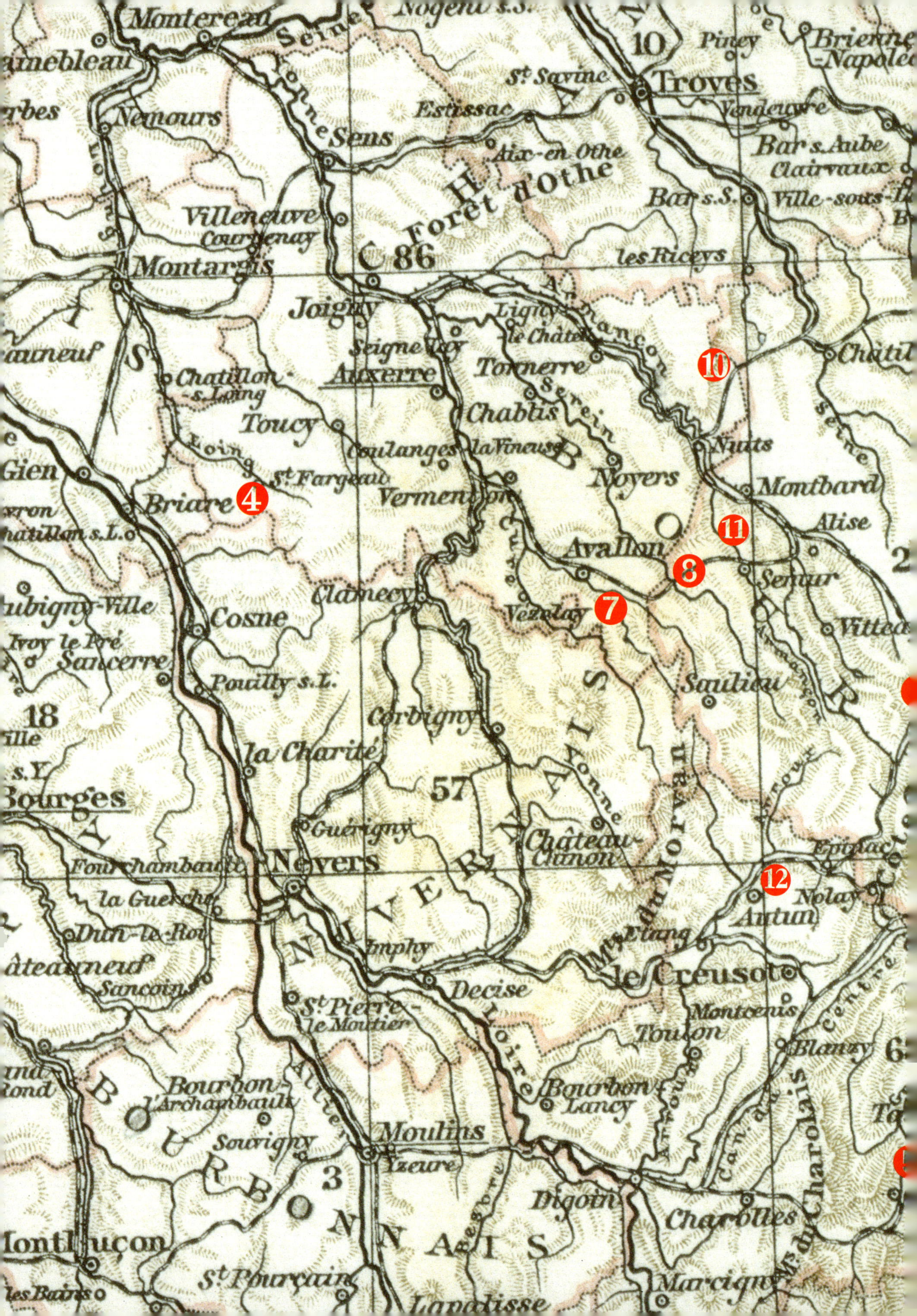

Montereau
Seine
Nogent s.S.
Piney
Brienne-Napoléon
10
Troyes
St Savine
Estissac
Vendeuvre
Nemours
Yonne
Sens
Aix-en-Othe
Bar s. Aube
Clairvaux
Forêt d'Othe
Bar s.S.
Ville-sous-la-F.
Villeneuve
Courtenay
Montargis
C 86
les Riceys
Joigny
Ligny le Châtel
Armançon
Seignelay
Auxerre
Tonnerre
10
Châtillon
Chatillon-s. Loing
Serein
Chablis
Toucy
Loing
Coulanges
la Vineuse
Noyers
Nuits
Gien
St Fargeau
Montbard
Briare
4
Vermenton
11
Alise
Avallon
8
Semur
Clamecy
Vezelay
7
Aubigny-Ville
Cosne
Ivoy le Pré
Sancerre
Pouilly s.L.
Saulieu
18
Corbigny
la Charité
57
Bourges
Guérigny
Château-Chinon
Fourchambault
Nevers
Epinac
12
Nolay
la Guerche
Autun
Dun-le-Roi
Imphy
Mts du Morvan
Mt Beuvray
le Creusot
Sancoins
Decise
St Pierre-le Moutier
Montcenis
Loire
Toulon
Blanzy
Bourbon-l'Archambault
Bourbon-Lancy
Souvigny
Moulins
Yzeure
3
Digoin
Charolles
Mts du Charolais
Montluçon
St Pourçain
Lapalisse
Marcigny
BOURBONNAIS
NIVERNAIS

Neufchâteau
52
Bourmont
Nijon
Chaumont-en-Bassigny
Nogent le Roi
Château-Villain
Langres
Bourbonne les Bains
Chalindrey
516
Le Fayl-Billot
Port d'Atelier
Champlitte
Thil-Châtel
Tille
3
Gray
Montagney
Dijon
Auxonne
la Barre
1
Nuits
Beaune
Saône
Dôle
Mouchard
Doubs
Arbois
Andelot
Poligny
Châlon s. Saône
Lons le Saunier
39
Seille
Louhans
St Amour
Mâcon

INFORMATION

1. Château of Clos de Vougeot - 21640 VOUGEOT

Category MH.
Open all year.
Receptions, exhibitions, and concerts.
Manager: Monsieur Claude Carlier.
Tel: 03.80.62.86.09
Fax: 03.80.62.82.75

2. Château of Rully - 71150 RULLY

Category ISMH. Member VMF and DH.
Open from 15 July to 14 September,
and all year by appointment for groups.
Owner: Monsieur Raoul d'Aviau de Ternay.
Tel: 03.85.87.13.10
Fax: 03.85.87.10.98

3. Château of Fontaine-Française - 21610 FONTAINE-FRANÇAISE

Category MH. Member VMF and DH.
Open from 15 May to 30 September.
Owner: Monsieur Xavier de Caumont La Force.
Tel: 03. 80.75.80.40
Fax: 03.80.75.80.40

4. Château of Saint-Fargeau - 89170 SAINT-FARGEAU

Category MH. Member VMF and DH.
Open from Palm Sunday to
11 November.
Historical pageant on Fridays
and Saturdays
in July and August.
Owner: Monsieur Michel Guyot.
Tel: 03.86.74.05.67
Fax: 03.86.74.18.63

5. Château of Cormatin - 71460 CORMATIN

Category MH.
Open 1 April to 1 November.
Owners: Anne-Marie Joly, Marc Simonet-Lenglart,
and Pierre Almendros.
Tel: 03.85.50.16.55. Fax: 03.85.50.72.06

6. Hôtel-Dieu in Beaune - 21200 BEAUNE

Category MH.
Open all year. 'Son et lumière' every
evening from April to November.
Owner: Hospices de Beaune.
Manager: Monsieur Jacquet.
Tel: 03.80.24.45.00
Fax: 03.80.24.45.99

7. Hôtellerie de Vézelay - CABALUS, rue Saint-Pierre, 89450 VEZELAY

Café gallery, bed and breakfast.
Tel: 03.86.33.20.66
Fax: 03 86.33.38.03
E-mail : cabalus@worldnet.fr

8. Château of Bourbilly - 21460 EPOISSES

Category ISMH. Member VMH and DH.
Open 1 July to 15 September, and from 1 April to 31 October for group visits.
Rooms for hire for receptions.
Owners: Monsieur et Madame Edouard de Crépy.
Tel: 03.80.97.05.02
Fax: 03.80.97.25.40

9. Château of Commarin - 21320 COMMARIN

Category MH. Member VMH and DH.
Open 1 April to 31 October.
Owners: Monsieur and Madame Louis de Vogüé
Tel: 03.80.49.23.67
Fax: 03.80.49.22.43

10. Château of Tanlay - 89340 TANLAY

Category MH. Member VMH and DH.
Open from Palm Sunday to 15 November.
Owner: Monsieur de La Chauvinière.
Tel: 03.86.75.70.61
Fax: 03.86.75.70.61

11. Château of Epoisses - 21460 EPOISSES

Category MH. Member VMH and DH.
Open in July and August. Groups by appointment only (with tasting of Epoisses cheese) from Easter to All Saints' Day (1 November). Park open all year.
Owner: Madame de Guitaut.
Tel: 03.80.96.40.56
Fax: 03.80.96.40.56

12. Château of Sully - 71360 SULLY

Category MH. Member DH.
Open every afternoon from June to October, and weekends and public holidays from Easter to the Hospices de Beaune wine auctions.
Room hire, bed and breakfast, gites, lunches, and dinners.
Owners: Monsieur and Madame de Mac-Mahon.
Tel. 03.85.82.10.27
Fax: 03.85.82.10.27

ABBREVIATIONS
MH : Monument Historique (listed historical monument)
ISMH : Inventaire Supplémentaire des Monuments Historiques (supplementary register of historical monuments)
VMF : Vieilles Maisons Française (old French houses)
DH : La Demeure Historique (stately home)

INDEX of recipes

GRAPHIC DESIGN
Brigitte Racine

Achevé d'imprimer en France par l'Imprimerie Mame à Tours (37)
I.S.B.N. 2.7373.2846.2 - Dépôt légal : février 2001
N° éditeur : 4222.03.03.04.06